The Philosophy of
Human Nature

The Philosophy of Human Nature

HOWARD P. KAINZ

OPEN COURT
Chicago and La Salle, Illinois

To order books from Open Court, call toll-free 1-800-815-2280, or visit our website at www.opencourtbooks.com.

Open Court Publishing Company is a division of Carus Publishing Company.

Library of Congress Cataloging-in-Publication Data

Kainz, Howard P.
    The philosophy of human nature / Howard P. Kainz.
      p. cm.
    Summary: "A philosophical analysis of the concept of human nature and controversies surrounding it" — Provided by publisher.
    Includes bibliographical references and index.
    ISBN-13: 978-0-8126-9619-6 (trade paper : alk. paper)
    ISBN-10: 0-8126-9619-0 (trade paper : alk. paper)
    1. Philosophical anthropology. 2. Human behavior. 3. Philosophy.
    4. Psychology I. Title.
    BD450.K279 2008
    128—dc2

                                          2008001593

Contents

Foreword

It has been said that philosophy can investigate, and tell us many things about, the *real world*—about matter, living things, animals, human beings, the angels, God—about anything and everything. Many of these things, including human beings, the subject of this book, are things in the *physical world*. And that is why they can be investigated by the sciences as well.

But philosophy can take us only so far, since philosophy does not use the methods of the sciences—controlled experiments, observational instruments, and measuring devices—which can take us quite a bit further. Together, philosophy and science can give us a *considerably more complete* account of things in the physical world than philosophy alone, or science alone. And not only that. They give us an account in which philosophy and science serve to help and to correct one another. This is what Professor Kainz has in mind as he writes, in his Introduction, that this book is an attempt at "coordinating philosophical analysis with the givens of empirical science," an attempt at "bringing about a rapprochement between traditional philosophy and empirical sciences." By "traditional philosophy" and "philosophical analysis" Professor Kainz means, as he explains, philosophy *prior to* the "existential phenomenology" of thinkers like Husserl, Heidegger, and others, whose writings emphasize subjective, or introspective, experience. This book, Professor Kainz points out, is closer in its approach to more *objective* systematic classical works, like the treatises on "Philosophical Anthropology" by Kant and Hegel.

In this book, Professor Kainz considers again, clarifies, and
brings up to date, what he did in his earlier book entitled *The
Philosophy of Man* (1981). Like that earlier book, The Philosophy
of Human Nature builds up very nicely, step by step, to what is no
doubt the most intriguing and haunting question about human
nature, the question of life after death. Though Professor Kainz's
book as a whole pursues the general question, 'What is human
nature?', it does so in terms of a number of specific questions, considered in Chapters 1 through 12.

How does human nature differ from the natures of other
things in the physical world? Are there instincts which are distinctively human? Are personality traits and intelligence inheritable?
Are male personalities significantly different from female personalities? And what about human evolution? Is it only biological, or
is it social and cultural as well? Is it based on an underlying cosmic evolution initiated by the Big Bang? Is human nature made
up of body and mind (soul)? Is the mind a *thing* in the sense in
which the body is a thing? Or is the mind some sort of *quality*,
produced by and retained by the body, in particular by the brain?
What is meant by "human freedom"? Are humans free? How do
humans develop from infancy into adolescence, and just beyond,
with respect to sensation, perception, memory, imagination,
understanding, volition, self-awareness, social sense, aesthetic
sense, ethical sense?

And what about human maturity? Is the mature person the one
who can avoid extremes as he moves into middle age, and then
into old age—extremes in his relation to physical things, to other
humans, and to himself? And what about love, and its various
kinds? What is the highest kind of human love? Are there human
powers which take humans in some way beyond loving, which
seems to be man's highest activity, and an activity of which *most*
humans are capable? Are there paranormal powers, at least in *some*
humans? What is the evidence, if any, for life after death? Near-
death experiences? A select group of mental operations which proceed in some way independently of the brain? Self-consciousness?
How are immortality and the resurrection of the body to be
understood? How are they related?

Professor Kainz's book takes a careful and sustained look at all these questions about human nature. To be sure, *not everyone* will agree with all of his conclusions. But everyone who reads this book, even half-attentively, will profit from it. The book is enjoyable from beginning to end. And instructive. Moreover, it opens many doors and windows to many further doors and windows. It is mind-expanding. It is liberating. One can very easily agree that what Gerald F. Kreyche says in his foreword to Professor Kainz's book of 1981 is just as true about the present book: that "he (Professor Kainz) leads, he encourages, but he never insists on having the last word, recognizing that it is the reader's right to make that judgment," and that he sets "a good example for others to follow in his honesty, his openness, and in his refusal to succumb to the temptation of simplistic answers."

Self-consciousness, as Professor Kainz maintains, may well be the essential difference-in-kind between human beings and other animals. It may even provide, one should note, the strongest evidence for survival of death. But self-consciousness, Professor Kainz observes in the Epilogue, is a very *complex* subject, and is beset with the *paradox* that whereas "it may be the most obvious to us, it is the least objectively observable and provable." But *all* the subjects pursued in this book are very complex—considerably more complex than the problems of mathematics, or of the physical sciences, or of the detective as he tries to track down the criminal—since they take into account and consider many subjective, or introspective, aspects which mathematics and the sciences and the detective must leave out, in order to arrive at the objective results which are their goal.

Human nature is complex beyond words, with the physical, the mental, and the spiritual encountering one another, and interacting, in a myriad of subtle and intricate ways. Philosophy has the difficult task of trying to understand this complexity. Professor Kainz's book is to be commended for making this task considerably less difficult.

JOSEPH BOBIK

Introduction

My first inclination is to entitle this book "philosophical anthropology"—which will in any case be its library classification. But I hesitate to do this, since the term "philosophical anthropology," is now used in a specialized sense. It has become largely synonymous with a group of philosophical efforts placed under the umbrella designation, "existential phenomenology"—works by Husserl, Heidegger, Merleau-Ponty, Buber, Sartre, and others. These works, quite different from one another in approach, do have some features in common. In the midst of the spread of totalitarian ideologies in the twentieth century, they responded by focusing on individual existence in the world as the starting point and the central issue for philosophical analysis. The keynote of such efforts has been the emphasis on introspective experience, and reliance on pure phenomenological analysis as a self-sufficient methodology. In existentialism and phenomenology, one finds occasional references to scientific developments—such as references by Sartre to Freudian psychology, or the general discussions of modern technology by Heidegger—but no major efforts to incorporate contemporary scientific data on human nature in any systematic way.

In twentieth-century Scholastic philosophy, based largely on the work of St. Thomas Aquinas (1225–1274), the branch of philosophy called "philosophical psychology" offered a different and somewhat systematic approach to questions about human nature. Metaphysical issues regarding human nature were considered—the relation of essence to existence in humans, the differentiation of essential from accidental properties, the functions of sensation, memory, imagination, intellection and volition, the faculties of the mind, freedom of the will, the immortality of the soul, and similar questions. But the empirical backdrop for the scholastic analyses was supplied by the biology, anthropology, and psychology of Aristotle. Contemporary scientific findings regarding human and animal traits, heredity, gender, emotions, social and cultural evolution, etc. were not considered as essential foci, and not systematically addressed.

Marching to a very different "drummer" than such philosophical approaches, sociobiologists, cognitive scientists, anthropologists, geneticists, psychologists and others have striven to bring empirical science to bear on questions about human nature. Steven Pinker's book, *The Blank Slate: The Modern Denial of Human Nature* is a noteworthy recent attempt to synthesize recent research in biology, anthropology, psychology and neurophysiology, throwing light on many contemporary issues, such as the "language instinct" in humans, IQ testing, worldwide moral universals, gender development, feminism, overpopulation distortions, sexual, moral and political implications of sociobiology, heritability, and modernist and post-modernist cultural developments.

But while Pinker hopes to avoid the pitfalls of "scientism" by incorporating insights from the arts and humanities, he flounders when he gets into the areas of philosophy and religion. Morality is reduced to optimistic sociobiological notions of kinship tendencies and group reciprocities; and Pinker never gets beyond what moral philosophers would call "descriptive ethics" to prescriptive or normative ethics. In pragmatic fashion, he addresses problems of responsibility by referring to society's ability to deter crime through suitable punishment (ignoring any questions about the moral responsibility of those who decide on the deterrents!). He dismisses freedom as a "ghost in the machine" concept, wasting his efforts on refuting a stereotypical, "straw man" notion of freedom as a power completely unaffected by any thing in the world. And he gives short shrift to God, who "has commanded people to . . . throw Protestants out of windows, withhold medicine from dying children, shoot up abortion clinics, hunt down Salman Rushdie, blow themselves up in marketplaces, and crash airplanes into sky-scrapers." God thus gives serious competition for sheer evil to atheists like Hitler, Stalin, Pol Pot and Mao Zedong!

In examining human nature, I will avoid such attempts to promote an ideological agenda. I believe the optimal stratagem is to steer a middle ground—avoiding a scientific approach which considers most traditional philosophy as irrelevant to an understanding of the issues, but also avoiding a philosophical approach which proceeds as if empirical science had nothing to offer for our understanding of human nature.

With the caveat that "classical" is not the same as "outdated," the philosophical anthropology in this book is closer in its approach to more objective systematic classical works—for example, Kant's *Anthropology in a Pragmatic Perspective* or Hegel's treatment of "Philosophical Anthropology" in his *Encyclopedia of the Philosophical Sciences*. Such works represent interesting efforts in the late eighteenth and late nineteenth centuries at coordinating philosophical analysis with the givens of empirical research, with regard to topics such as: the specific difference between humans and other animals, the classification of personalities, the connection of ethnic and racial differences with geographical or environmental conditions, gender differences, the stages of human development, the "unconscious," hypnotism, mental diseases, and the nature of mind and imagination. Of course, the science of that era included many things that most would consider passé in science now—the four-temperament theory, Mesmerism, Eurocentric theories of ethnic and racial characteristics, phrenology, physiognomy, and so forth. Psychology and anthropology have progressed considerably since then, and possibly many of the results of these sciences will *not* be passé two hundred years from now. So it appears worthwhile to make similar efforts in what Kant and Hegel called "philosophical anthropology," following their lead in bringing about a rapprochement between traditional philosophy and empirical sciences.

My methodology in treating of the topics in this book combines historical perspectives with appeals to ordinary experience as well as to relevant scientific developments, and with conceptual analysis. The order of the topics is not arbitrary, but rationally linked, such that each topic leads into the next, and each problem calls for clarification of a sub-problem. In brief, the linkage proceeds as follows in the following twelve chapters: (1) In trying to pinpoint any essential and crucial differences between humans and the other animals, we cannot ignore (2) the widespread consensus that humans, unlike animals, are not ruled by instinct; but (3) if there are any innate, instinctive or non-instinctive human traits, they have to be understood in terms of the dynamic interrelationship of heredity and environment; obviously, (4) our concepts of male and female are one major result of that interaction, and the current status of gender roles needs examination; but (5) our fuller understanding of both males and females leads us to focus on the larger context of evolution, especially social and cultural evolution, which has led in recent centuries to a heightened emphasis on individuality and personality; but (6) when we discuss personality, is the traditional distinction between mind and body still relevant, or do we need to change paradigms? and (7) our response to this question will inevitably have an impact on our concept of the freedom (or lack of it) of embodied beings; any balanced notion of freedom, however, requires (8) a complementary acknowledgment of the necessities and determinacies that affect every person in development from infancy, and (9) if the stages of human development have any teleology, the concept of human maturity needs to be considered; (10) the ability to love is commonly taken as the acme of normal human maturity, and needs philosophical analysis as much as knowledge and other normal human abilities; but (11) is there any evidence for the existence of *para*normal abilities, such as ESP, in some or perhaps all humans? and finally, (12) the currently most discussed and most heavily documented "paranormal" experience (NDEs) leads us naturally to a reexamination of the perennial question in all cultures and religions about the possibility of survival after death. As we consider these final issues, we will see that they were already implicit in the "difference" question with which we started.

In my book, *Paradox, Dialectic, and System* (1987), I argued that the tendency of mainstream philosophers to avoid (or "solve" or rebut) paradoxes may be a mistake; it may be the case that the sort of questions that philosophy is asking may be best answered by paradoxical formulations rather than straightforward quasi-syllogistic conclusions. In the conclusion to this book, I have gathered up for inspection a few of the paradoxes that have emerged from our examination of the specific topics we have considered. At this point I will be satisfied with the relatively tame paradox that to undertake the critical investigation of characteristics of human nature is itself a major characteristic of human nature.

1

The "Difference Question"

In the great majority of animals there are traces of psychical qualities which are more markedly differentiated in the case of human beings. For just as we pointed out resemblances in the physical organs, so in a number of animals we observe gentleness or fierceness, mildness or cross temper, courage or timidity, fear or confidence, high spirit or low cunning, and, with regard to intelligence, something equivalent to sagacity. Some of these qualities in man, as compared with the corresponding qualities in animals, differ only quantitatively: that is to say, a man has more of this quality, and an animal has more of some other; other qualities in man are represented by analogous qualities: for instance, just as in man we find knowledge, wisdom, and sagacity, so in certain animals there exists some other natural capacity akin to these.

—ARISTOTLE, *History of Animals*

Of course, if apes could speak our special place in the universe would be imperiled, but the cardinal de Polignac [1661–1742], for one, felt no real danger to his faith when he approached the chimpanzee in the glass cage at the *Jardin du roi* and proclaimed "Parle, et je te baptise" ["Speak, and I will baptize you"].

—ROBERT WOKLER, *The Ape Debates in Enlightenment Anthropology*

1

Once we allow that there really is something called "human nature," an unavoidable question about the difference between human beings and the other animals arises. We start thinking, "maple trees have a cluster of characteristics connected with their 'nature'; and the same goes for dogs, and gold and lead; human beings should have certain unique characteristics connected with their nature . . . shouldn't they?" And the next logical question is: "if that is the case, then what *is* their special characteristic? Or what *are* these special characteristics? And, in particular, how do they differ from the animals considered most similar to humans?

What can philosophy contribute to the solution of such questions? It is sometimes said that philosophy doesn't primarily provide us with new knowledge, but makes us conscious of knowledge we all possess already. For example, we all know what is meant by "being," "causality," "mind," "evil," "right and wrong." But if we are challenged: "Just what do you mean by "being," "right," and the rest, we might not have a ready answer. This could be the case with the question about human differences: possibly we know the answer already, but are not yet able to articulate it clearly, in such a way that someone will not counter with the remark, "but animals have that same quality or capability."

But some "differences" are different from others. An important initial distinction has to be made between "difference in degree" and "difference in kind." If A and B are different in *degree*, this means that fundamentally the same characteristic is found in A and in B, but to a different degree. For example, a hawk and a blackbird and an owl can be said to differ in the quality of their eyesight; a lion and a horse and an ostrich differ in running speed; many animals differ in their powers of hearing. Schematically, we might present these differences as a comparison of $A(x)$ and $B(x')$, to show that two animals, A and B, have a similar capacities, but to a different degree (x as contrasted with x').

However, if we say that A and B differ in *kind*, we mean that some important, essential characteristic exists in A that is never found in B. For example, we might be referring to the type of reproduction found in mammals, as compared with the way that birds reproduce; or the mode of breathing in reptiles as compared with fish; or possibly the "radar" of bats compared with the senses of other animals. Schematically, the difference here can be formulated as a comparison of A(x) with B(y), where the variable, y, is used to indicate the more radical difference in the capacities of animals A and B.

Our main interest in this chapter is the second type of difference, difference in kind. Thus, when we ask the "difference" question here, we are asking, "is there any essential, important characteristic in man, that is not found to *any* degree in animals. We are not interested in differences in seeing, hearing, and the like.

As you might expect, many philosophers have attempted to address this challenging question. We will start with a sampling of theories from some influential philosophers:

1.1 Some Philosophical Approaches

(1) The ancient Greek philosopher, Aristotle (384–322 B.C.), gave a variety of answers:

Rationality. The two main meanings which "rationality" has for us are a) the ability to make mental connections between causes and effects, between means and ends; and b) the ability to control our inclinations, passions, and so on, instead of being controlled by them. The first of these meanings has a theoretical orientation, the second emphasizes practical aspects. Both of these meanings are recognized as valid and important by Aristotle. In asserting that human beings are "rational" animals, he is claiming that other animals lack the ability to connect effects with their causes and choose appropriate means to achieve ends, and also that these other animals, unlike humans, are completely controlled by their inclinations or natural tendencies.

Reminiscence. Reminiscence or "recollection" is distinguished from "memory" by Aristotle. The faculty of memory enables us to focus on images as past, for example images of places where I have lived or people I have known. Reminiscence is more complex: It has to do with the power of sifting through our store of memories in a systematic way to locate a certain image which is not immediately accessible to memory. For example, I cannot find my coat or my wallet, so I go back in my memories of previous events and activities and locations until I recall a place where I last took off my jacket to hang it up, or last took out my wallet to pay a bill. According to Aristotle, this is a specifically human ability, not imitable by any animal.

The "political instinct." Aristotle characterized human beings as social/political animals. Living in society and constructing communities, cities and states, is not just an accidental feature of some humans, but a distinguishing factor which is not present in the other animals. Aristotle concluded that an individual who did not need or want the society of other individuals must be either a subhuman beast or superhuman and godlike.

Risibility. Risibility—a sense of humor, and the ability to laugh—are also strictly human characteristics, according to Aristotle. Animals may do things that appear funny to us, and laughing hyenas may make sounds that sound like human laughing, but animals themselves have no sense of humor, can't make jokes, and certainly don't laugh at their own jokes.

Featherless biped. Aristotle, concentrating on biological classification in terms of genus and species, said that humans in relationship to other animals might be classified as the only featherless bipeds. Whether or not there are other two-footed animals without feathers (kangaroos? "Bigfoot"?), Aristotle in his zoological observations was not aware of them, and thought he was safe in making this generalization.

(2) The influential German idealist, Georg Wilhelm Friedrich Hegel (1770–1831), thought that the main difference between us and the other animals was in regard to needs. Animals may have many needs, but they are always limited according to their species; humans, however, have an infinite number of needs—not just natural needs, but artificial needs that we create for ourselves and that keep multiplying. This, if it is true, is good news for the advertising profession. According to Hegel, even if one had everything (for example, won the $250 million lottery), he or she still wouldn't be satisfied, and new needs would continue to arise.

(3) At the turn of the century, Friedrich Nietzsche (1844–1900), focused on the orientation of the human species toward future

progression, and differentiated human beings from animals by their ability to "promise for the future." Nietzsche's conclusion was that animals are locked into the present, and into meeting present needs, but humans have the ability to plan and make commitments for the future, sometimes even the very distant future. Thus they demonstrate the power of *will*, by which they have evolved to superior status among the animal species.

(4) However, Ernst Cassirer (1874–1945), called the "philosopher of culture," insisted that the most important difference separating human beings from the other animals was in symbolization. Human beings, according to Cassirer, are the only animals who can make and use symbols. We create words, signs, icons, and other forms of symbolization; we live on the level of symbols, and deal with the world and other people in and through symbols. This is a "second-order" relationship to reality, one step removed from the first-order level of direct acquaintance with the sensible world. Animals, in contrast, live strictly on that first-order level.

1.2 Critique of These Historical Approaches

(1) Aristotle's observations touch on some important human characteristics, but do they really focus on the most important differences?

Rationality in our time, as well as Aristotle's time, is often characterized as a specific, or *the* specific quality of human beings, distinguishing them from animals, who are irrational or at least subrational. With regard to *theoretical reasoning*, it seems clear to us that animals don't have the ability to perform complex mathematical operations or construct arguments or narratives. But isn't this just a difference of *degree*, rather than a difference in *kind*? The American philosopher and psychologist William James (1842–1910) in his *Psychology* relates the example of a hunting dog, whose job it was to retrieve still-living birds shot down by his master. One day two birds were shot, but still living. Hunting dogs do not usually kill the prey being hunted. But in this case cited by James, the dog killed one of the birds to keep it from escaping, and then brought the living bird to his master before returning to the dead bird. This of course is not an example of advanced powers of deliberation, but demonstrates something like the ability to connect specific causes with specific effects. We also hear of tool-making tests carried out with animals—for example, monkeys putting together segments of interlocking poles in order to reach bananas too high to be reached, gorillas stripping leaves from twigs to fish for termites, chimps using rocks to crack nuts open. If reasoning in its *theoretical* aspect involves an understanding of the relationship of means to ends, it seems that animals can make some basic rational connections.

Similarly, with regard to *practical* reason, or "will," the supposed power of humans to channel inclinations and control passions is also subject to doubt. If we consider the bloodbaths, terroristic and genocidal acts that have sullied twentieth-century history—the holocaust in Nazi Germany, Stalinist purges in the USSR, death squads murdering street children in Colombia, intertribal massacres in Somalia and Ruanda, "ethnic cleansing" in Bosnia, suicide bombers indiscriminately murdering innocent civilians in the Middle East, and so on—we might hesitate to insist on any human superiority in this regard. The record of the relationship of animals to members of their own species is quite a bit better in this regard! If we focus just on *capacities*, we might argue that humans have *potentially* greater ability to exercise rational control over emotions and passions; but if the issue is *actual control*, we must concede either that reason often fails to subdue inclination or passion, or that human reason itself has been frequently inhumane.

Reminiscence. A homing pigeon, in finding its way back to the location where it was released, will initially make wide arcs, which become narrower and narrower as it gets closer to its destination. This appears to parallel quite nicely the process that a human goes through, in trying to remember a previous event or fact—looking initially over wide expanses of time to determine the best possibilities, then zeroing in on specific places and times to focus on the relevant details. A human, like the homing pigeon, will sometimes even move around physically from place to place, looking for clues, although the mental operations are the most important and advanced "movements" connected with reminiscence.

The Political Instinct. We know that many primates—for example, apes—and many other animals, establish hierarchies in which those at the top are given greater access to food and mates, and take on leadership roles in conflicts or in migrations to other territories. One of the most basic examples of hierarchical subordination among animals is the "pecking order" common among hens—where hen A acquires the right to peck hen B without being pecked in return, and hen B acquires similar right over hen C (sometimes hen C may acquire the same right over hen A—leading to a "vicious circle"). Can we say that any significant difference exists between these mechanisms and what takes place at various levels in corporations (immortalized in the comic strip, *Dilbert*), or even, for that matter, in a university?

Risibility. Animals of course lack vocal powers for laughing, aside from vocalizations by "laughing hyenas" that mimic human laughing; but animal owners often report that their pets play practical jokes on them, and look forward to playing games with them. Even if these activities do not constitute a sense of humor in the strict sense, however, we may have doubts about the importance of risibility as a defining characteristic. Would we want to say that the great distinction of human beings is due primarily to the fact that they are "laughing animals"? Arguably this is an important characteristic; but even Aristotle did not point to it as the defining characteristic, but rather as one interesting human property.

"Featherless bipedialism." Aristotle no doubt demonstrated his own sense of humor in pointing to this as a basic human characteristic; and he may have been unaware of some possible exceptions. This description is comparable to the descriptions of *Homo sapiens* (offered to us by anthropologists and paleontologists) as the species that rose above quadrumanosity (four-handedness) to achieve technical progress by using the thumb and opposing finger. "Featherless biped" is probably a valid generalization about mammals (kangaroos might be one exception), but in any case it is obviously not an essential characteristic pinpointing the difference of human nature from animal natures.

(2) Marx *versus* Hegel. Karl Marx (1818–1883), a student of Hegel, initially developed communist political theory through an extensive critique of Hegel's political and social philosophy. In response to Hegel's observation about the human characteristic of "infinitely multiplying needs," Marx agrees that this is the case at present, but relates this to capitalistic economic mechanisms. The "genius" of capitalism, in other words, is to continually create artificial needs to induce consumers to buy more and more unnecessary products, and thus create markets for the wares of the capitalists, constantly increasing pressures on overworked and underpaid workers. Communism, in contrast, Marx hypothesized, would encourage people to cultivate their real needs, in particular the need for other people, a need which is unfortunately ignored because of the pressures of capitalist competition.

(3) Nietzsche. One need not look too far to find counter-examples to Nietzsche's contention that humans are uniquely distinguished by their ability to make commitments for the future. We often hear of the extraordinary faithfulness of dogs to their masters, who are certain they can rely on these animals, without any spoken or written assurances, for future help. Those who shrug about this, and refer it to a "meal ticket" syndrome, need to explain why dogs sometimes will be willing to sacrifice their life to save their masters from danger. Some species of birds which mate for life offer another example of commitment of animals among themselves—in comparison with which the divorce rate for married humans might engender doubts about the human capability for commitment.

(4) Cassirer. One of the chief examples of the use of symbols by animals is found in the observation of the habits of bees. A bee scouting for sources of honey will return to its hive and announce the amount of available pollen or nectar by the vigor of her dance; the distance, by the number of turns per minute; and the direction, by zigzagging horizontally, vertically, or diagonally with respect to the position of the sun. There can be no doubt that the bee is using symbols for communication.

In recent decades, animal researchers have also tried to determine whether animals are capable of using human language symbols. Studies carried out at the Yerkes Regional Primate Center in Atlanta, Georgia, with a chimpanzee named Lana, indicated some successes in the early 1970s, teaching Lana to punch out words and sentences on a computer keyboard. Lana learned to use lexigrams in phrases to communicate with trainers, saying for example, "Please machine give M&M," "Please machine make window open," and so forth. Two subsequent chimpanzees, Sherman and Austin, used such symbols to communicate with each other, as well as humans. They attained vocabularies of 50–150 symbols, joined in communications, sent simple messages to each other, and combined symbolic messages with nonverbal gestures. Such apparent successes were challenged, however, by critics who suggested that the trainers, if not fraudulently hiding unwelcome results, were unintentionally giving cues to the animals, followed up with rewards like food or playing. In the absence of proper controls, they objected, the animals were not really learning the meanings of words, but only performing in a way that would please their trainers and result in rewards. In response to such criticisms, however, researchers began to tighten up their methods in order to avoid pure stimulus-response mechanisms. Sue Savage-Rumbaugh and other researchers have given special attention to Kanzi, a bonobo ape, who without any training began to pick up language from his adoptive mother, Matata, while Matata was undergoing training from Savage-Rumbaugh. When researchers realized that Kanzi had learned twelve symbols by watching and listening, and was able to use these symbols in 120 utterances, they began to train him. They claim that at nine years of age he was able to respond appropriately to 72 percent of 660 directions given by researchers behind a one-way mirror. For example, he was able to respond appropriately to directions such as "give the doggie some yogurt," "go scare Matata with the snake," "put on the monster mask and scare Linda." (Other experimenters in the room with Kanzi, wearing earphones playing loud music, videotaped Kanzi's responses.) As a control on these experiments, a child $2\frac{1}{2}$ years of age, named Alia, was given the same directions and responded appropriately to 66 percent of the directions.

The results of these experiments seem to indicate that animals can be taught to use language with grammar and syntax at about the level of a toddler, and to communicate in an elementary way with humans and possibly other animals. Would Cassirer have to revise his theory? Cassirer might concede that such achievements give us some evidence that animals can *use* symbols that they are taught by humans; but evidence of animals actually *creating* symbols is consistently lacking; the symbols are supplied to the animals by the researchers. Finally, and most importantly, he would notice that in all these experiments animals are using language just to *do* things (to carry out commands or requests, or get items they need or want, or get the attention of trainers). What is conspicuously absent—and seems hardly likely to turn up—is the ability to speak about their own thoughts—for example, to refer to their own mental representation of "machine," "snake," "Matata," and so forth, or to explain to a fellow animal what they mean by a certain sign or lexigram.

1.3 Distinctive Human Conceit?

Before we proceed any further, we might pause to consider a possibility that hasn't been suggested by any of our authorities: Might we not say that the claim that human nature is different in kind from the nature of animals is just a case of human conceit? Could it be that the claim of "distinctiveness" is just one more example of self-serving hubris on the part of our species—a claim in the same genre as the boasting of aristocrats or upper-class people to be of "higher quality"? In this case, the "distinction" would be reducible to the fact that our particular species claimed to be distinct, claimed to be something "special," while the other species, in a more humble vein, do not show any particular interest in making such claims!

But while this may explain the motivation of some people, something more fundamental is taking place: The human conviction of being "distinctive" seems to be a symptom or side-effect of heightened self-consciousness; and this brings us to a consideration of human self-consciousness itself for a possible solution to such questions.

1.4 The Importance of Being Self-Conscious

There does appear to be at least one strong candidate for the honor of being the "x-quality" that finally differentiates human beings from all the other animals—namely, self-consciousness. Apes and some other primates show an ability to recognize themselves in a mirror, thus showing a consciousness of their own body. Human infants around the age of nine months show a similar ability, but in normal development will be able to progress to self-consciousness in a literal sense—consciousness of one's *self* as the center of conscious activity—the ability not just to know, but to know that they know; not just to think, but to think about their thinking and about the contents of their thought. This power, with which thought circles back upon itself, appears to offer us the most promising solution to the "difference" question.

For (1) it seems to be responsible for some of the other characteristics discussed above. For instance, both the operations of "reminiscence" and the ability to make "promises for the future" appear to presuppose the ability to reflect upon one's own experiences and capabilities; such operations are obviously external manifestations of prior acts of reflection.

(2) It seems obvious that animals don't sit back and reflect on themselves or their thoughts. We cannot get inside the skin of animals, and all our judgments are based on inferences from their external actions and reactions. But the fact that animals like Kanzi, who can be taught to use words for external things, cannot refer to their own mental representations, seems to indicate that they lack reflexive ability. Someone who objects, "How can you be sure my cat does not have the power of self-reflection?" has obviously been overly influenced by comic strips in which dogs and cats and other animals are routinely anthropomorphized to act and talk like humans.

(3) The final argument in favor of this solution is more complex, subtle, and even paradoxical: The operations of self-consciousness necessarily involve a psychic withdrawal—a withdrawal into oneself. This withdrawal-into-self is at one and the same time a self-*distinction*—by which I shut out, or bracket out, all other things and persons for the moment, as I circle back on my own

thoughts. Self-consciousness of its very nature is the *act* of distinguishing oneself from everything outside the self. Thus it would be nonsensical to ask a person during the act of self-reflection, "By the way, do you think you can distinguish yourself from the animals?" The self-reflecting individual *is* distinguishing himself from animals (and other things) *in thought*, and it is precisely this special power of reflexive thought that is his best claim to being essentially different or distinctive among animals.

This solution, of course, necessarily depends on our subjective intuition of our own powers of self-consciousness. This subjectivistic approach, externally unobservable, and thus lacking scientific verification, may be considered a weakness. If a more external, objective proof is required, one final "last-ditch" possibility suggests itself: We might consider the final, clear-cut distinction of humans from the other animals as a *future* event. Let us suppose—as is quite probable, since the species *Homo sapiens* presumably has millions of generations ahead of it in evolution—that the real difference between humans and the animals hasn't yet become *manifest*. Let us consider the possibility that, in spite of all contemporary evidence to the contrary, a moral evolution is taking place. Consider the positives: In the last few centuries the human species has arrived at the point where slavery is no longer condoned by civilized peoples; the world has definitely gotten beyond accepting practices of public child sacrifice; and hasn't a significant part of the world finally risen to the realization of the evils of torture, child labor, and the systematic oppression of women? In the future, as we evolve further in brain capacity, social refinement, and political organization, there may be no more wars, no more genocide, no more injustice, no more terrorism. We may approximate to the biblical ideal enunciated by the prophet Isaiah, "converting swords into plowshares," to inaugurate a final state of peace and justice. If that happens, the difference between us and the other animals will be so obvious that you would be ashamed to ask the "difference" question. On the other hand, if the *opposite* happens, then, in the midst of rampant unrefined animality, the question will also disappear of its own accord, and our philosophical "last-ditch" effort will have become obviously irrelevant.

2

Are There Any Distinctively Human Instincts?

A social instinct is implanted in all men by nature, and yet he who first founded the state was the greatest of benefactors. For man, when perfected, is the best of animals, but, when separated from law and justice, he is the worst of all.

—ARISTOTLE, *Politics*

Some cognitive scientists have described language as a psychological faculty, a mental organ, a neural system, and a computational module. But I prefer the admittedly quaint term "instinct." It conveys the idea that people know how to talk in more or less the sense that spiders know how to spin webs.

—STEPHEN PINKER, *The Language Instinct*

The great decisions of human life have as a rule far more to do with the instincts and other mysterious unconscious factors than with conscious will and well-meaning reasonableness.

—CARL JUNG, *Modern Man in Search of a Soul*

The *Encyclopaedia Britannica* defines instinct as "a largely inheritable and unalterable tendency of an organism to make a complex and specific response to environmental stimuli without involving reason." Human beings generally pride themselves on their rational capacities, and would not like to think of themselves as engaging in behavior—especially very complex behavior—"without involving reason." But this presupposition needs re-examination.

We take for granted that animals have evolved some remarkable automatic behavior mechanisms that have helped their species to survive. Salmon fight their way upstream and climb up waterfalls to arrive at their birthplace to reproduce; beavers inspect woods, cut timber, build dams in streams and habitations for themselves, showing considerable engineering skills; the weaver bird builds a nest with an antechamber, entrance tunnel, egg chamber and roof; some types of bats catch flying insects by using Doppler sonar; various species of animals engage in highly stylized dancing and ritual behavior before mating.

It is generally acknowledged that there are some relatively simple instincts that humans have in common with animals—for example, the sucking instinct, which a nursing mother doesn't have to teach to a hungry newborn; and it is sometimes observed that teenagers have something similar to the herd instinct found in some mammals. It has even been suggested that humans may have, in common with animals, a complex instinct for hierarchical social rankings—a fact which might have important negative implications for socialist, communist, and other egalitarian movements, if they gravitate toward the extreme of a "classless society." But are there any important, distinctively human instincts, that we don't have in common with animals? Some philosophers and psychologists have theorized that human beings have instincts peculiar to their species.

2.1 Some Historical Positions

Virtue as instinctive. Plato (428–348 B.C.), after a rather lengthy discussion in the *Meno* about whether virtue can be taught, comes to the tentative conclusion that "virtue is neither natural nor acquired, but an instinct given by God to the virtuous. Nor is the instinct of virtue accompanied by reason, unless there may be supposed to be among statesmen some one who is capable of educating statesmen [to be virtuous]"—a possibility which Plato recognizes, but considers rather unlikely. What Plato appears to be referring to is "natural virtue"—a quality which leads some people to instinctively "do the right thing." St. Thomas Aquinas (1225–1274) theorized that there was something similar in humans to the *vis aestimativa* (instinct) of animals, except that human instinct (the *vis cogitativa*) is related to the benefit of the individual, while animal instinct is oriented toward the survival of the species. Just as lambs will flee instinctively from wolves, and young animals will instinctively avoid poison mushrooms, so also every human has an emotionally based intuition of what is injurious to himself or herself as an individual. Aquinas, as a theologian, pointed out obstacles to the working of this intuition because of "original sin," but asserted that the *vis cogitativa* was a natural faculty that was still operative in individual natures. In modern philosophy, the "moral-sense" theories of third Earl of Shaftesbury (1671–1713), Francis Hutcheson (1694–1746), and David Hume (1711–1776), although they do not make explicit reference, like Plato, to instinct, are similar insofar as they connect virtue with "fellow-feeling," natural sympathy and empathy.

Subject-object differentiation as instinctive. Hegel (1770–1831) theorized about an "instinct of reason"—a conception of reason and "rationality" that goes beyond Aristotle's notion. Hegel is referring to the tendency of consciousness (also noted by child psychologists in studies of infant development) to differentiate itself from the external world, to distinguish subject from object, and then to engage in constant efforts to co-ordinate the two sides, showing the relationship of being to thought and vice versa, and also to discover the intellectual and spiritual areas where an interface between being and thought takes place.

Creativity as instinctive. Henri Bergson (1859–1941) wrote *Creative Evolution*, a book that described a progressive impetus of evolving life to produce creative breakthroughs, both in the theoretical sphere and in practical affairs. Going beyond Darwinian concepts of "natural selection," he suggested that an instinctive process called "intellectual intuition" was necessary to explain the new creative insights in science and the humanities, as well as in political and social developments, that drive mankind forward.

Instinctive Eros. The psychoanalytic theory of Sigmund Freud (1856–1939) originally proposed the sex instinct, or "libido" (also characterized as the "life-instinct" and "Eros") as the springboard for human ego-development. In his mature works, Freud coupled this very generalized erotic instinct with an instinct for aggression (the "death-instinct" or "Thanatos"). According to Freud, the proper channeling of Eros leads not only to healthy sexual relationships but also to aesthetic "sublimations" of the sexual instinct, such as art and music, and movements toward social and political unification as "erotic" developments in the wide sense; while the proper channeling of aggression takes place through work and through displaced and non-lethal forms of aggression, such as sports.

The instinct to learn. Maria Montessori (1870–1952) founded an innovative system of elementary schooling which has spread throughout the world. The philosophy of education which she developed in numerous writings promotes an approach that builds on a child's natural instincts to work and to learn—which like all instincts, can be misdirected or thwarted without the proper environment. Montessori education emphasizes constructing a learning environment utilizing materials which in conjunction with the highly individualized approach of the teacher will be most conducive to furthering these instincts. The basic assumption is that the child does not have to be taught to learn, and is able to teach himself or herself, if the proper conditions are provided; and that using the wrong pedagogical methods may inhibit or repress the instinct to learn.

2.2 Complex Instincts in Humans?

The theories just discussed are interesting, and possibly valid. But after considering them, one might observe: none of these theories appear to be concerned with *predictable and complex* instincts—

there seems to be nothing comparable to the chained operations carried out by the beaver in building a domicile, by the bee in signaling the location of pollen, or even the spider in constructing a web. As an example of extreme complexity, consider the larval stage of the Capricorn Beetle: Initially the thin larva burrows through the trunk of an oak tree, gradually increasing in diameter and making a tunnel as the wood it eats is expelled. It gets to the bark, deposits a thin membrane, and then retreats to create a chamber big enough for a beetle. It seals up the chamber and builds a concave cover for it. The larva then sheds its skin, becomes a pupa, and finally a beetle, which pushes aside the cover, goes through the opening, breaks through the bark membrane and exits from the tree.

Considering such intricately interwoven behaviors, we are told that there are no important and complex instincts ruling human behavior, since our species has gotten beyond such built-in "hardwiring." We human beings, it is said, reason things out, make changes in our environment, change our social behavior when necessary. The absence of instinct, the fact that we are not "programmed" to carry out specific serial operations, is supposed to be the key to understanding the infinite variability and unpredictability of human behavior.

But is this really the case? Before going any further, we should note that we face two significant obstacles in the investigation of this problem: (1) The concept of instinct is *ambiguous.* Sometimes descriptions/definitions of instinct are given in terms of "innate neuromuscular mechanisms" or internal "arousal"; at other times a list of basic habitual actions or behaviors is made, the emphasis being on the observable externals. As an analogous case, "love" often refers to an internal emotion; but we also refer to external acts as "love"—for example, sexual intercourse, kissing, hugging. In both cases, if the usage is not clear from the context, ambiguity may result. (2) An even more formidable obstacle is the problem of *objectivity.* If we were governed to a considerable extent by a complex instinct, would be able to recognize it for what it is? Given that we characteristically pride ourselves on *freedom* from instinct, would we be willing to admit that we are controlled by instincts in any important fashion—even, perhaps, in areas where we take pride in our abilities to control, to organize?

(1) A way to overcome the above-mentioned problem of *ambiguity* is to clearly differentiate the two types of instinct. In what follows, I will use the term, *Cognitive Instinct*, to refer to the internal processes that may be instinctive in human nature; while the term, *Behavioral Instinct*, will refer to observable human instinctive acts or responses. A *complex* cognitive instinct in human beings would refer to an intricate mesh or network of internal conscious or unconscious mechanisms, while a *complex* behavioral instinct would refer to a chained series of externally observable human activities.

(2) With regard to the problem of *objectivity*, no easy solution is at hand. An analogy with hypnotism may be helpful: A hypnotized subject—say, in a stage demonstration or under the care of a psychiatric practitioner—will sometimes carry out some complex instructions suggested by the hypnotist; but, if asked "why are you doing this?" while carrying out these instructions, will not say something like, "oh, because I'm hypnotized!" Instead, if the subject answers this question at all, he or she will typically offer some rationalization, indicating some personal choice made, but not implicating the hypnotist. So also, a human being under the influence of an instinct, carrying out complex instructions programmed into the genes, would presumably react in a similar way, with rationalizations, denying that he is being controlled in any way.

It is possible, however, that self-consciousness itself may provide the solution for this obstacle. Just as, in the infrequent cases of self-hypnosis (autosuggestion) an individual can conceivably be in a state in which one's hypnotic state is not completely unrecognized, but semi-conscious, a person with heightened self-consciousness, on the lookout for controlling complex instinctive activities, may be able to recognize and account for such activities. Let us hope that this is a possibility, as we examine the following two possibilities of a complex instinct found in all humans, but in no subhuman species.

2.3 Human Cognitive Instinct

The theory of Carl Gustav Jung (1875–1965) concerning the *Archetypes of the Unconscious* offers us the best candidate for a complex cognitive instinct. According to Jung, human beings have, below the level of the conscious psyche, both a personal unconscious, consisting of forgotten or repressed images of experiences, and also a "collective unconscious," an inherited repository of patterns which influence the way we formulate our developing consciousness of the world. In other words, our mind is not a *tabula rasa*, a blank tablet upon which impressions are just received and imbedded from outside, but is endowed with instinctive tendencies for making sense out of the world, just as animals are equipped with instincts enhancing their chances of survival and development. According to Jung, the evidence for the existence of preprogrammed archetypes in the human unconscious is to be found a) in dreams, including occasional powerful dreams which leave a lasting impression on our memories; b) in psychopathological conditions such as schizophrenia, in which archetypal images sometimes appear; and c) in folklore, legends and religious traditions throughout history in the world as a whole, in which some symbols and images keep reappearing. Jung also finds evidence for the reappearance of archetypes in modern literature and art.

The chief archetypes relevant not only to the understanding of cultures, but also to individual psychological maturation, include the following:

(1) *The persona*, the "mask" that we put on in response to the demands of our social environment; this is the way we want to appear to other people, and it is often divergent from one's actual conscious state. Our self-concept may or may not reflect any discrepancy between the persona and the self.

(2) *The shadow*, our "dark side" that we would not want to become recognized by others, and that we would like to avoid encountering in ourselves. Much of our conscious activity and thinking may be understood as an attempt to escape from our dark side, or from what we consider our dark side to be. But the shadow may be "projected" on to other people, to whom we react with

hostility or fascination, depending on the status of our own personal self-integration. The shadow also appears in literature in depictions of character conflict, and in the simplified form of classical villains.

(3) *The anima*, the eternal feminine. In Jung's psychology, the human psyche is essentially bisexual, but as one's persona is being formed in masculine or feminine ways, the converse (feminine or masculine) characteristics, because of social expectations, hormonal predominance, and so forth, are repressed to one's personal unconscious. The archetype of the anima from the collective unconscious influences the formation of these personal unconscious images; and typically in the masculine psyche the notion of the ideal woman will be developed. This ideal affects sexual attraction, insofar as some females become "carriers" of the projected image. Jung theorized that variations on this process of development, in which a male would identify with the anima, instead of repressing it, could result in homosexuality; and treatment in Jungian psychoanalysis for homosexuality often involves application of this theory.

(4) *The animus*, the eternal masculine. This is the counterpart of the anima, typically developing in the female, in which the strength of the archetype would influence the personal formation of unconscious notions of the ideal male. Variations on this development, according to Jungian theory, would also help explain homosexuality in females.

(5) *The self* is the most important of all archetypes, being the image of integration of opposites—anima and animus, persona and shadow—and being the key to the mature development of the individual, often delayed to middle age or beyond. Besides being the unconscious impetus to personal integration, the self-archetype is portrayed externally in various religions as circles, "mandalas," and other symbols, and in Christianity is the subjective basis for the iconic power of the Christ-figure.

These archetypes, together with other archetypes (the Wise Old Man, the Earth Mother, and others) are influenced by our culture, religion, and social environment, as far as regards the various concrete ways they are reflected in dreams and external "projections";

but the initial, general impetus and directions are provided by the instinctive apparatus shared by all humans in their collective unconscious. Thus, according to Jung, we inherit a complex repertoire of basic patterns for understanding the world, but specific contents for these patterns are supplied from our interactions with our environment.

2.4 Human Behavioral Instinct

How do we learn language? Here again, we can ask the *tabula rasa* question: Is the mind of a child like a blank tablet that receives all sorts of impressions from outside, then proceeds to store these impressions, along with rules governing them, and apply them in future experiences? According to Noam Chomsky, this model would never explain the acquisition of language by human beings, bombarded with all kinds of grammatical and ungrammatical sentences from birth; an instinctive orientation toward producing language has to be presupposed. Just as an instinct enables a bird to build a nest or to sing a song that is characteristic of its species, so also human beings are endowed with an instinct for "universal grammar," which enables them to comprehend the basic rules for grammar and syntax in their language, and also learn other languages. For example, in English there are many words that have multiple meanings, or can be used as nouns or verbs—"bank your money" versus "swim near the bank"; "jump over the fence" versus "give the car a jump"; "never lie" versus "you need to lie down"; "pool your resources" versus "let's play pool" or "jump in the pool"; "the teachers work" versus "the teachers' work" or "the teacher's work"; and so forth. In colloquialisms, we instinctively refrain from expressions that would be confusing. For example, if we are in the process of choosing teams for a volleyball game, after team captains have already been chosen, someone might say to one of the captains, "who do you wanna choose?"—where "choose" is used as a transitive verb; but if it was a matter of electing two captains to do the choosing, that same person, even though no purist in verbal expression, would instinctively avoid the elision of "want to" into "wanna"; he or she would say, "who do you want to choose?"—where the verb "choose" is used intransitively.

If Chomsky is right, one implication of his theory for education would be that students should be exposed to language-learning at the earliest age possible, before they have developed ingrained habits in a "mother tongue." Exposed to instruction in different languages and peer groups with varying languages, a child becomes bilingual or trilingual without great concentration efforts, moving easily from one language set to another—putting the verb after the object in German, learning to use nouns without articles in Russian, differentiating words by tone or pitch of voice in Chinese, and so on.

Numerous software programs are currently available, enabling users to translate texts from one language to another. However, these programs use hundreds of rules to help identify the special syntax connected with each language. Using Chomsky's principles, Robert Berwick and his colleagues at the Massachusetts Institute of Technology Artificial Intelligence Laboratory have been able to identify about twenty-five grammatical rules for analyzing all major languages. Using their computer program, a person can type in a sentence from many languages, with a few simple instructions, and get a precise grammatical analysis of the language in question. This analysis, however, is concerned only with the basic *form* of the language; it does not offer any translation of the content, since "universal grammar" is only concerned with the formal structures, the patterns which people instinctively pick up in languages—the position of verbs, nouns, prepositions, qualifiers, and so on.

Chomsky's critics sometimes point out that current research traces back all extant languages to a proto-language that emerged in Africa over fifty thousand years ago. They argue that this origin indicates that a long series of experiences and adaptations, instead of an instinct, is the more probable explanation for the multiplicity of languages that have developed in our world. But Chomsky's question would be: if that is true, how did it originally develop in Africa, if not instinctively?

The difficulty of answering this question is just one more indication of the special difficulty which attaches to any discussion of complex human instincts. If we were "programmed" by certain instincts, would we be able to recognize them for what they are? Or do they necessarily belong to a part of our "unconscious" which resists being made conscious? If Jung is right, some of our basic attitudes towards friends and enemies, men and women, as well as our self-concept and attitude towards religions, are influenced by inherited predispositions that have been built up over numerous generations. If Chomsky is correct, in our use of language we are not just following rules we have learnt in school, or acquired from our social and cultural environment, but adhere to unlearned, instinctive guidelines while we are speaking or writing, in order to make our points clearly and effectively.

3

Can Personality Traits and Intelligence Be Inherited?

No man is voluntarily bad; but the bad become bad by reason of an ill disposition of the body and bad education. . . . And in the case of pain too in like manner the soul suffers much evil from the body. Further, when to this evil constitution of body evil forms of government are added and evil discourses are uttered in private as well as in public, and no sort of instruction is given in youth to cure these evils, then all of us who become bad become bad from two causes [evil constitution of the body, and bad environment] which are entirely beyond our control. . . . But . . . we should endeavor as far as we can by education... to avoid vice and attain virtue.

—PLATO, *Timaeus*

A capacity for one-sidedness . . . bids us to observe things from one angle only, and if possible to reduce them to a single principle. In psychology this attitude inevitably leads to explanations in terms of one particular bias. For instance, in a case of marked extroversion the whole of the psyche is traced back to environmental influences, while in introversion it is traced back to the hereditary psychophysical disposition.

—CARL JUNG, *Flying Saucers: A Modern Myth of Things Seen in the Skies.*

In our preceding discussion of instinct, we have conveniently omitted any extensive analysis of environmental factors. But instincts, simple or complex, as well as other inherited tendencies or traits, require the proper environment in order to be activated; otherwise specific instincts may be blocked or diverted. For instance, if a bird does not have proper nest-building materials, it will either improvise or do without a nest; bees will not perform their waggle dance to indicate the direction and distance of nectar, unless food supplies are in the environment; and foxes who are caged in a zoo will develop trotting circuits around their cage, since they are prevented from the instinctive hunting of prey. Likewise, if Jung's theory is correct, the archetype of the "Self" will be stimulated and take on different content, depending on the religious or cultural figures and expressions which it encounters in the environment; and the fact that feral children (rare cases of children raised by wolves or other animals from infancy for a number of years) cannot be taught language, may be taken as evidence that the "universal grammar" theorized by Chomsky would require proper environmental stimulation in order to be activated.

This brings us to the general problem of the relationship of heredity to environment, or what is often called the "nature-nurture" problem, first posed explicitly 2,500 years ago by Plato, trying to explain in his *Timaeus* why people turn out morally good or morally evil. Plato's explanation in terms of "disposition of the body" and "education" may appear a bit simplistic to us—even a combination of "good genes" (nature) plus the right type of government and educational facilities (nurture) may not be sufficient to produce a good human being; and good human beings may emerge when either or both of these factors are deficient. In other words, we might want to add "freedom" or "personal choice" as a third factor; and a Christian might suggest that "grace" or "divine assistance" could change the moral equation considerably. But it seems clear that the interaction of heredity and environment is of fundamental importance for determining the development of personality and possibly even for conditioning intelligence or moral character. Current controversies generally have to do with the relative weight to be assigned to the two factors, heredity and environment; but the importance of heredity is the most controverted topic of all.

3.1 Heredity

The science of genetics is one of the "new kids on the block" in the neighborhood of science. Some basic ideas of how characteristics could be transmitted in plants and animals were understood in the nineteenth century, but most of what we now know about biological inheritance of traits and characteristics are the result of discoveries during the twentieth century. There are some certainties, some areas of probability, and some controversial or doubtful areas.

The certainties we have are mostly with regard to strictly biological characteristics—color of eyes, skin, hair, and the like, and also susceptibility to diseases, such as diabetes, colon cancer, high blood pressure, hemophilia, sickle cell anemia, Alzheimer's disease and cystic fibrosis. Some nervous or mental disorders which are triggered by physiological conditions can also be classified as inheritable—for example, manic-depressive psychosis (bipolar disorder), which is associated with a chronic deficiency of a mineral (lithium), and Huntington's disease, a slow disintegration of the brain brought on by a genetic "marker" inherited from a parent. Insofar as basic temperamental orientations, such as extroversion and introversion, have a biological basis, they are also considered inheritable.

But there still are many areas of uncertainty, especially with regard to the inheritability of personal and mental characteristics. Possibly future genetic research will offer some solutions to the questions we have about such characteristics, but the solutions are likely to be controversial, since the science of genetics tends to elicit controversies even more than other sciences.

3.2 The Past and Present of Genetics

The *past* of the science of genetics is unfortunately littered with racism, ethnocentrism, and class prejudices. For example, Francis Galton, a cousin of the evolutionist Charles Darwin, published a book entitled *Hereditary Genius* in 1868. This book contained plans for improving the intelligence of the general population, and reducing the number of misfits and defectives, through "eugenics" (a new term coined by Galton). The interest in the "science" of eugenics mushroomed, and led in the 1920s to the establishment of the American Eugenics Society, a WASP organization notable for emphasizing the superiority of "Aryans" over blacks, Jews, Catholics, and Southern European immigrants. Also, not coincidentally, Margaret Sanger founded Planned Parenthood in order to help reduce the number of "defectives" and produce "a race of thoroughbreds" through birth control; and the science of psychometrics blossomed with the development by Lewis Terman of the Terman IQ test, created to help identify the "1,000 gifted children of the 1920s." In the late 1920s, sterilization laws were enacted in twenty-four states. Sterilization of defectives was especially rampant in California, and helped to inspire Nazi experiments with eugenics a decade later. More recently, a gentler form of the eugenics movement (PRAM, the "Pregnancy Risk Assessment Monitoring System") has emerged offering "Norplant" programs in thirty-one states for giving contraceptive implants, lasting five years, to selected subjects. Governmental incentives have also been offered in other countries. For instance, in accord with 1987 eugenic laws, the then Prime Minister of Singapore, Lee Kuan Yew, offered grants for the education of children of educated women, and grants for the sterilization of uneducated women; a government agency in Singapore, the SDU (Social Development Unit), is still heavily engaged in helping single educated males and females find suitable mates.

The most notable *present* example of the progress of genetic science (hopefully neutral toward eugenics) is the recently completed Genome Project, a project inaugurated by the United States Congress in 1988, and funded by the Federal Government, with collaborative efforts by foreign governments and scientists in Japan, the United Kingdom, Italy, France and Russia. The objective of the Genome Project has been to map all the genes in the human body—thus making possible some understanding of the statistical relationship of the genes to inherited diseases and/or inherited traits, although the gene's effect on inheritance can't be predicted just from knowing its place in the nucleotide sequence. The beneficial possibilities of this project have been hailed by physicians, but possible deleterious collateral effects have also raised fears on the part of ethicists. What might result, for example, if parents acquire knowledge not only (as at present) of the sex of a fetus, and a few disease prognoses, but of the fetus's susceptibility to a wide range of physical and mental diseases, or IQ, or criminality? Are we really prepared to have experts and prospective parents making judgments about who are "defectives," and ultimately offering advice or making decisions about whether "defectives" are to be born or not—for example, if genetic tests indicate that a fetus has a thirty-percent probability of being born physically or mentally deficient? If the past is any prologue to the future, it would seem that a tremendous increase in abortions will result. For we are like the characters in Garrison Keillor's *Lake Wobegon*, searching for a social environment in which "all the men are strong, all the women are beautiful, and all the children are above average" (or like college administrators who would prefer all their professors to achieve "above average" scores on their teaching evaluations?).

3.3 The Problem of Isolating Variables

The answer to Plato's problem about the influence of nature and nurture, and subsequent offshoots of that problem, would be significantly simplified if we were able to pinpoint just what is contributed by hereditary components in individuals, as contrasted with what is contributed by environmental factors. In some simple living species, this separation of hereditary and environmental variables has actually been accomplished. The best-known example is the case of the Drosophila fruit fly, where relatively accurate predictions of the number of eye-facets can be made, if geneticists have information about environmental variables such as temperature, and hereditary variables such as whether a fruit fly is type A or B—two types which have differing sensitivities to cold and heat.

More eye facets	Medium amount	Less eye facets
Type A fly has generally more		Type B fly has generally less
Cold temperatures increase eye facets for both Type A and Type B		Warm temperatures decrease eye facets for both Type A and Type B
Cold temperatures affect Type A even more than Type B		Cold temperatures affect Type B less than type A
	Warm temperatures do not have as much effect as cold on either Type A or Type B	

TABLE 3.1 Factors Affecting Amount of Eye Facets of Drosophila Fruit Fly

A geneticist with information about all these variables could make some accurate predictions about the number of eye facets in selected groups. And in principle, if geneticists knew all the hundreds of environmental and hereditary variables that are associated with some specific human trait or ability, they might be able to make fairly accurate predictions of the relevant probabilities, just as we do with the drosophila fruit fly. But only "in principle," since even with the most advanced computer program, we would hardly know what variables to input and how to weight this or that variable. Thus at present we are confronted with quite a few controversial areas, where we would have difficulty applying Plato's nature-nurture principle with any hope of accuracy, although proponents do exist on both the nature and the nurture sides who claim to have relatively clear and unambiguous answers.

3.4 Contemporary Areas of Controversy

(1) *Homosexuality.* It is of course clear the true homosexuals are not going to pass on their genes to their offspring! But there could possibly exist hereditary transmission from bisexuals, or as a recessive gene from heterosexuals. Some studies by endocrinologists indicate a correlation of hormonal factors (for example, the ratio of androsterone to etiocholanolane) to habitual sexual orientations; anomalies in DNA patterns on X chromosomes of homosexual brothers were found in one study; and some disparities in the size of the hypothalamus in gay men have also been claimed. Such evidence would bolster arguments that homosexuality is inherited rather than environmentally induced. But studies of identical twins separated at birth have been inconclusive, and the "gay gene" reportedly detected in 1993 by Dr. Dean Hamer has been called into question by further Canadian studies.

In 1973 the American Psychiatric Association reclassified homosexuality from a "mental-health" problem to normality. But Dr. Robert Spitzer, who led the movement at that time for reclassification, reported at the 2001 APA conference that he has had considerable success in helping homosexuals change their sexual preference. The reported "cures" of homosexuals by some psychiatrists raise questions, of course, about whether their patients were "true" homosexuals in the first place. In psychiatric practice since the mid 1970s, practitioners who interpret homosexuality as an inherited condition may tend to see homosexuality as a problem only in the sense of finding personal identity and integration, especially if a homosexual faces a homophobic social environment; while those who believe it is environmentally induced tend to treat it as a "problem" susceptible of cure. For example, some recent studies indicate that the probability of homosexuality in a male increases statistically with the increase in the number of older brothers. But we should keep in mind that environmentally induced homosexuality *may* be incurable, and genetically transmitted homosexuality *may* be susceptible of treatment.

(2) *Schizophrenia.* Experts are divided regarding the source of schizophrenic "voices" and delusions, and thus are also divided

regarding the proper approach to treatment or cure of this mental disease. Psychoanalysts have traditionally presumed that past influences from family and others have affected the unconscious of the schizophrenic patient, and they have thus approached treatment with "talk therapy," dream analysis, free association of words, and so forth. Psychiatrists, capitalizing on the success of psychotropic drugs, often tend to rely on specific pharmaceuticals to "control" schizophrenic symptoms, although they make no claims of cures, and in many cases no satisfactory explanation is available about why a treatment "works." A clear-cut understanding of whether the source of schizophrenia is environmental or genetic would privilege one of these therapeutic approaches over the other.

(3) *Intelligence—due to Heredity or Environment?* The notion that intelligence is inherited is best illustrated by some of the extreme measures which have been employed to "produce" more intelligent babies. One of the most egregious examples is the "Genius Farm," established by Robert Klark Graham (who died in 1997) in Escondido, California. Graham (like Prime Minister Yew, mentioned above) was responding to the alleged problem that people of superior intelligence were using birth control, while inferior people were reproducing themselves (and their inferiority) shamelessly—a process that, in Graham's estimation, led to the downfall of the Roman Empire, and is destined to lead to the demise of our civilization. Graham's genetic solution: to collect the sperm of Nobel Laureates, to be used for artificial insemination of women who were members of Mensa (an organization exclusively for people at or above the 99th percentile of the population in I.Q.). Only three Nobel Prize winners contributed their sperm, so Graham adjusted the requirements for males in terms of "significant scholarship." As of 1995, approximately two hundred children had been born using this procedure, and many of them tested out with a high I.Q. This result does not actually prove Graham's thesis, however, since it is quite probable that the children were raised in a high I.Q. family, and environmental variables have not been isolated from possible hereditary influences. It is also possible that an environmentalist (someone who emphasizes the influence of environment on personality instead of heredity)

might want to start an alternative "Genius Farm" providing the best possible intellectual environment, and achieve similar or even better results.

Racial IQ controversies—from Jensen to Rushton. The watershed for some continuing controversies regarding the interrelationship of race and I.Q. was an article published by Arthur Jensen in the late 1960s in the *Harvard Educational Review*. Jensen focused primarily on the fact that "culture fair" I.Q. tests—in which by removing "culture-loaded" questions from I.Q. tests, a particular group is brought up to the average I.Q. of 100—had been successfully developed for the males and females and for all major groups, but not for blacks, despite repeated efforts. Jensen's conclusion was that, although individual blacks could attain the highest I.Q. levels, efforts to raise the level of intelligence of blacks as a group through government programs (such as the Head Start program) were doomed to failure. William Shockley, recipient of the Nobel Prize for his work in transistor technology (and also the first to contribute his sperm to Robert Klark Graham's Genius Farm) aroused considerable controversy in the 1970s by spreading Jensen's ideas on college campuses, and also suggesting a system of rewards for sterilization reminiscent of the Singapore system mentioned above. During the 1990s, a very similar controversy has developed, fomented by Part III of *The Bell Curve* (1994), a book published by Charles Murray and the late Richard Herrnstein, and also by *Race, Evolution, and Behavior* (1995), by J. Philippe Rushton, a Canadian, leading to cover stories in *Newsweek*, *The New Republic*, and *The New York Times Book Review*, a special section in *Current Anthropology* (February 1996), as well as articles in other magazines and newspapers, including black magazines like *Jet* and *Essence*. Murray, Herrnstein, and Rushton have carried Jensen's argument further with attempts to refine the psychological and sociological controls, incorporation of studies on identical twins, and cross-cultural comparisons including studies from Asia, Europe and Africa. They also widened the parameters of racial difference, by concluding that Asians as a group had a higher IQ level than whites, and that Ashkenazi Jews as a group were a standard deviation higher than whites statistically, just as whites were a standard deviation higher than blacks.

More recent advances in psychometrics have let to concentration on the "*g* factor" rather than IQ scores. The *g* factor is defined as a general factor common to a large number of IQ tests, and is arrived at by comparison of various IQ tests and giving different weight to items within these tests. The theory is that some items are more "*g*-weighted" than others. For example, questions about spatial patterns, are said to give a better prediction of cognitive ability than some other questions; and questions measuring inductive or deductive reasoning are "g-loaded," as well as items measuring verbal ability and mathematical ability. Most psychometricians now consider the *g* factor a more accurate indication of cognitive ability than IQ. Tests which are said to be "highly *g*-loaded" include the Stanford-Binet Intelligence Scale, the Wechsler Intelligence Scale for Children, and the Raven Progressive Matrices. In response to these developments in psychometrics, Arthur Jensen, whose article initially ignited the race and IQ controversy in the sixties, published a book in 1998, *The G Factor*, which focuses on *g* rather than IQ, and concludes with social and political recommendations more moderate than those he offered in his earlier study.

Voices of opposition. In 1996 the American Psychological Association, responding to the controversy emerging from the publication of *The Bell Curve*, agreed that genetic factors do influence IQ, and that IQ differentials among groups are not necessarily the result of biases in test construction or differences in socio-economic status. But numerous psychologists, psychometrists, and sociologists have reacted to the allegations of racial differentials in IQ, arguing that environmental factors were not taken sufficiently into account, that the investigative methodology was faulty, and that data from racist publications have been utilized (attention has been focused especially on the journal, *Mankind Quarterly*, financed by the Pioneer Fund, which has had a racist and white-supremacist history). The "Flynn effect," discovered by James R. Flynn, is often cited: namely, that there has been a +.2 increase in I.Q. scores among test-takers every year for about the last 50 years throughout the world. For example, Americans who are measured at an IQ of 100 now would get a score of about 114, if they took the 1949 test! In his more recent work, Flynn accounts for such paradoxical results: No, it is not the case that generations are simply getting smarter (improvement of genes); and no, the "Flynn effect" is not simply due to environmental changes. What has happened is that performance on certain valid g elements of IQ tests, such as "similarities" subtests and other tests that focus more on abstract or formal types of intelligence rather than concrete and practical types, has undergone constant and remarkable improvement, thus raising the overall g rating of a particular population. These specific noteworthy improvements can be explained by the way that natural intelligence (even of identical twins separated at birth) in effect "chooses" or even brings about a certain preferred environment, and also by "environmental" developments that have become commonplace in the social world since the industrial revolution—in particular, the rise of scientific ways of looking at the world and the habits of categorization that these bring about.

Steven Jay Gould in *The Mismeasure of Man* claims that racist conceptions still motivate much IQ testing, and argues that there is a conceptual fallacy in the use of factor-analysis for the assessment of general intelligence; and Howard Gardner in *Frames of Mind* argues that the notion of a g factor is flawed because all creative and intellectual work takes place within various "domains" which call for diverse types of intelligence. Gardner maintains that there are at least seven types of intelligence: linguistic, as exemplified in a poet like T.S. Eliot; logical-mathematical (Einstein as an example); spatial (exemplified in an artist like Picasso); musical (the composer, Stravinsky, as an example); bodily-kinesthetic (for example, the dancer Martha Graham); intrapersonal (for example, the psychoanalyst Sigmund Freud); and interpersonal (exemplified in the political charisma of Mahatma Gandhi). Gardner's thesis illustrates the suspicion emerging among many psychometicians regarding the measurability, and even the existence, of a "general intelligence."

On the other hand, completely abolishing tests of general intelligence, as some of the critics have proposed, may be an exercise in "throwing out the baby with the bathwater." For one thing, the fact that there are certain specific or more focused areas of intelligence does not necessarily mean that these areas do not coexist with a more general form of intelligence. We should also remember that at the beginning of IQ testing, many educators, sociologists, and psychologists saw these tests as instruments for identifying and offering extra assistance to gifted youngsters who were handicapped by economic and social circumstances. As long as this approach makes no distinctions as to race, ethnicity, or other group identifications, it seems that IQ tests can be, and have been, useful for assuring that everyone will have the necessary resources for working at his or her capacity. This important function of the testing should not be obscured by racial-IQ debates, if indeed, as the psychometric community still insists, *g*-loaded tests can give us some reliable assessments of cognitive ability.

(4) *Sociobiology (a.k.a. "Evolutionary Psychology"): Sex, marriage, and kinship patterns.* Edward Wilson, a Harvard entomologist specializing in the effect of genes on ant-behavior, became interested in an apparent gap in Darwin's theory of evolution. The Darwinian principle of natural selection through the "struggle for survival" helped to explain the existence of most species and the extinction of some species, but seemed to fall short in explaining apparently *altruistic* types of behaviors. For example, squirrels may warn about the arrival of hawks at the risk of their own life; male baboons will help other males to fight off a mating competitor, then leave without receiving any benefit; some ants, bees, and rodents devote their lives to the offspring of others, and give up their own chance to reproduce. The theory of the "selfish gene" leading to constant competition for food and other resources, and competition to outproduce other species, just did not account for such behaviors. Wilson's 1975 book, *Sociobiology: The New Synthesis* was an attempt to address this mystery for animal behavior in general, to explain not only the origin of traits such as territoriality, xenophobia, and aggressive instincts, but also tendencies to make sacrifices for conspecifics, sometimes leading even to loss of an animal's own life. Richard Dawkins's 1976 book, *The Selfish Gene*, contributed to further emergence of the sociobiological approach and the solution to the problem of altruistic behavior in

animals. But Wilson and the sociobiologists following his lead have not hesitated to apply his theories also to *human* behavior. They use theories based on gene-transmission from our hunter-gatherer ancestors to argue that ethics should be biologically based. They are often vague about what the biological/ethical rules should be, beyond kinship loyalties and the willingness to extend altruism to wider horizons; but sometimes more specific applications are made. For example, Michael Levin in a 1984 article in the philosophical journal, *The Monist,* used sociobiological principles in great detail to argue that homosexuality is unethical, or biologically abnormal. Sociobiologists have also dared to enter into the field of gender issues, offering biological reasons for the more promiscuous sexual behavior of males as compared with the "coyness" of females, and the strong female orientation toward family stability and "domesticity"; the preference of males for younger females, and the male emphasis on personal assurance of paternity; the greater emphasis of males in prestige and recognition, and the like. More adventurous researchers have even offered sociobiological explanations for the greater number of men than women as CEOs, for the greater investment by parents in their female children than in their male children, and for peoples' kindness to complete strangers.

It should come as no great surprise that sociobiological theory, which seems to be saying that humans are "hardwired" toward certain types of behavior, has incited opposing forces. The main reactions against sociobiology have been from three groups: from ethicists, who maintain that *facts* about biology, even if valid, can tell us nothing about moral *values*, that is, norms concerning right or wrong; from scientists such as Stephen Jay Gould and Richard Lewontin, who perceive sociobiology as a threat to social and political change; and from feminists, who perceive sociobiology as a renewed attempt to gain acceptance for the "anatomy is destiny" principle associated with Freud and others. In the face of such criticisms, sociobiologists have modified some of their more exaggerated claims, started to refer to their discipline as "evolutionary psychology" rather than "sociobiology," and attained respectability sufficient enough for the Darwinist John Alcock to publish a book in 2001 on *The Triumph of Sociobiology*. In any case, the controversy regarding sociobiology is an important contemporary example of the continual reappearance of the classical nature-nurture questions posed by Plato, and, along with disputes about racial IQ, leads us to two considerations—one political and one social—that help to put the problem in perspective and even suggest a paradoxical solution:

3.5 The Political Paradox: Some Ironies in Democracy

We should realize that environment-heredity problems are not just purely scientific puzzles, capable of being solved objectively with standard scientific methods. In particular, the unavoidable connection of such problems with issues of democracy must be understood. If, for example, we consider the emergence of a new democracy like the United States in the eighteenth century, throwing off its British royalist origins, one would expect the resulting political system to be intellectually "environmentalist" (emphasizing environmental conditioning, instead of heredity). The problem faced both in the American and the French revolutions was "blue blood"—the presupposition that members of royalty and the aristocracy had superior traits and values that raised them above the masses, and that they were capable of passing on these natural, inherited advantages and prerogatives and preferences to their descendants, who were in general "good stock," "quality" individuals. Political power was essentially a hegemony of a minority of empowered people, who maintained their position by genetic transmission to legitimate heirs, often the first-born son. But democracy was the new "idea whose time had come," that challenged the equilibrium of these patterns. The whole thrust of democratic institutions was to do away with special inherited privileges, and "level the playing field," opening up positions of power and influence and leadership to all, no matter what their ancestry. Thus in the French Revolution, the major goal was to reduce the "Three Estates" (clergy, nobles, and commoners) to one estate; in the aftermath of successes in the American Revolution, George Washington rebuffed efforts among officers in the Continental

Army to make him a king; and after Independence the United States Constitution resolutely prohibited any titles of nobility. In the nineteenth century, Karl Marx in his *Critique of Hegel's Philosophy of Right* argued that he was bringing democracy to its logical conclusion by advocating a truly classless society, through the communist ideal.

As it turned out, democracy found itself in an ironical position—needing to systematically downplay and even ignore "natural endowments" of any kind, including leadership traits, in order to build a society with maximum mobility and opportunities for all. This unspoken principle has become a guiding beacon in the social sciences and psychological sciences operating in a democratic context. Even though the principle of "value-free" objectivity is sacrosanct in such sciences, a strong and recurrent distrust remains about analyses of personality traits, character, interpersonal relations, and so forth, that use "nature" or "inborn tendencies" as explanatory devices. Thus theories concerning genetic causes of intelligence, or sociobiological explanations of morals and mores encounter resistance based not just on scientific considerations, but also on political commitments. And if, as recent studies in behavior genetics indicate, liberal and conservative political attitudes have a significant genetic component, the complications become more difficult to disentangle. If theories emphasizing hereditary factors are wrong, the wrongness may itself be a consequence of environmental pressures on theorists from other members of the elite group to which they belong. If the theories are right, the rightness may be challenged because of political commitments which view the theories as incompatible with democracy; and these political commitments *may* themselves be genetically conditioned, if, as Jung asserts, introverts tend to look for hereditary explanations while extroverts tend to focus on environmental conditions.

3.6 Dobzhansky's Social Paradox

Theodosius Dobzhansky in *Man Evolving*, takes these ironical considerations to their logical conclusion with some reflections pertinent to the caste system in India, but capable of wider application, as will be shown.

In pre-modern India the caste system was a rigid stratification, affecting every individual and every pursuit or occupation in society. The social tiers of this system, ranging from the lowest rank of the "Untouchables" to the high, priestly rank of "Brahmins," with intermediate warrior and business classes, is outlawed in modern India, but residues of caste are still widespread in an unofficial way, influencing education, careers, social mobility, and even marital choices. For example, matrimonial advertisements in Indian newspapers and websites usually specify the caste of the person who is looking for a mate, and the "acceptable" caste of the prospective mate.

Dobzhansky suggests that the initial motivation for a caste system, besides the obvious desires for maintaining power and wealth, may have been the intention of preserving the perceived superiority of the upper class—what we might call now, in biological parlance, "preserving superior genes." Let us hypothesize, Dobzhansky continues, that the Brahmins initially *did* have strong claims to superiority in intelligence, leadership ability, physical fitness, psychological maturity, and so on, and that they had an understandable wish to preserve these qualities in posterity, keeping inferiors or misfits out of their class by strict social and political structuring.

Such a plan, although apparently rational, was doomed to failure, observes Dobzhansky. For if we analyze the situation a little further, we find that the higher castes kept all kinds of inferior people in the "superior" caste out of caste-loyalty, because they were brothers, sons, fathers-in-law, or other relations; and, since historically the higher-caste men had habits of patronizing lower-caste prostitutes or concubines, without any possibility of socially-approved marriage or a permanent union, they were in effect just passing on their "superior" genes to the lower classes. Thus, after a number of generations, all that would remain would be a distant memory of genetic superiority. The highest caste, continually promoting the fortunes of incompetent siblings and uncles, would have diluted its gene pool to such an extent that it could no longer boast any special natural superiority; the lower caste benefitting from the superior genes passed on to their females would eventually have "leveled the playing field" genetically. Although the higher castes continued to maintain the caste system by force for their own advantage, any initial justification for starting the caste system would have vanished centuries ago. Such considerations led Dobzhansky to a paradoxical solution: Granted that it may not be very humane or conscientious to consider one's kinship group superior, nevertheless if this group *had* significant superiority, and if one *wished* to maintain it in the best possible way, then the only way to accomplish this would be to do away with the caste system to allow maximum mobility upward and downward—so that inferior people in the higher classes could descend to their own proper level, so to speak, and superior people in the lower classes could enter the higher classes, and even intermarry with members of the highest class.

Some obvious applications of this general principle suggest themselves: In contemporary culture we encounter factual situations in which members of some groups have considered themselves naturally superior to other groups—white supremacists versus blacks; Nazis versus Jews; Zionists versus Palestinians; Australian whites versus aborigines; Irish "Orange Men" versus Irish Catholics, and vice versa. The immediate "gut" impulse of the self-described "superior" group has always been to maintain the sense of superiority by keeping separate from the alleged "inferior" group and not allowing incursion of individuals from that group into their own superior group. But as Dobzhansky's Paradox shows, this strategy has little probability of working, and will never confirm the type of certainty about superiority that they are seeking. Ironically, in order to achieve this sort of certainty, the alleged "superior" group would have to allow maximum mobility to members of the alleged "inferior" group, to see over a sufficiently long time whether they show the general incompetence that they are supposed to have; and members of the superior group would have to be allowed, if they wish, to marry members of the inferior group, to see, over the period of several generations, whether or not the offspring turn out to be markedly inferior because of dilution of the gene pool. It might turn out, as a result of this genetic "affirmative action," that the superiority of the group doing the testing would be proved, and the consequent certainty they have would be a justified certainty. But then again, the results may be just the opposite. No one who is for some reason interested in knowing about group superiority will be able to know, without such testing.

A testing of sexism (defined as a certainty of male superiority vs. females) is also susceptible to such testing, *minus*, of course, the intermarriage directives—no pattern of male restrictions on marrying females is associated with sexism! In other words, it is only after allowing maximum mobility over many years to females to enter into traditionally male bastions of power, that a sexist male could have any valid verification of male superiority.

4

Are There Any Significant Sex-Related Personality Charactersitics?

We must throw open the debate to anyone who wishes either in jest or in earnest to raise the question whether female human nature is capable of sharing with the male all tasks or none at all, or some but not others. . . . If it appears that the male and the female sex have distinct qualifications for any arts or pursuits, we shall affirm that they ought to be assigned respectively to each. But if it appears that they differ only in just this respect that the female bears and the male begets, we shall say that no proof has yet been produced that the woman differs from the man for our purposes, but we shall continue to think that our guardians and their wives ought to follow the same pursuits.

—Plato, *Republic*

No one can safely pronounce that if women's nature were left to choose its direction as freely as men's, and if no artificial bent were attempted to be given to it except that required by the conditions of human society, and given to both sexes alike, there would be any material difference, or perhaps any difference at all, in the character and capacities which would unfold themselves.

—John Stuart Mill, *On the Subjection of Women*

I will start by playing "devil's advocate." Granted, if any *hereditary* gender attributes exist, we should not overemphasize them in such a way as to stifle creativity and freedom. It would be a mistake for anyone to say or think or believe, "because you are male, or female, such-and-such is normal behavior for you, you should have this sort of tendencies, and act in this sort of way." Sigmund Freud's dictum, "anatomy is destiny," leaves no room for freedom and creativity, and would be disastrous if put into practice literally. Nevertheless, freedom and personal choice do not exist in a vacuum; if we were to conduct a philosophical analysis of the human person without taking into account gender, we may be missing important or even indispensable factors.

For example, in recent decades there have been movements to avoid common stereotypes in raising children (blue colors for boys, pink for girls; short hair for boys, long for girls; trucks and cars and blocks as toys for boys, dolls and toy houses for girls; and so forth). Many parents have become involved officially or informally in these movements, but with mixed results. In addition to anecdotal evidence, controlled psychological and sociological studies have been conducted. In a 1975 study of ninety-six middle-class girls and boys between the ages of one and six, 375 vehicles were found in forty-eight boys' rooms, only seventeen in the girls' rooms; and only four of the boys had a doll, while over fifty percent of the girls had a doll. Is this due to the fact that parents or caretakers were consciously or unconsciously reinforcing cultural stereotypes? Or to peer pressure? Or to the influence of advertisers and marketers? Even professional researchers who consider themselves 'progressive' in regard to gender differences, have been surprised at the appearance of sex-specific traits in spite of their best efforts to discourage the stereotypes. Could it be that even well-meaning and educated persons, and progressive parents, are fighting an ideological battle that is sure to be lost because of factual aspects of the "human condition"?

4.1 Biological Differentiation of the Sexes

In the beginning of fetal development no noticeable sexual difference can be discerned. If a three-week old fetus were inspected visually, it would not be possible to tell its sex. Up to three months, the fetus is basically bisexual in internal and external organs, with femininity as the default sex. A gradual increase of androgen over estrogen (or vice versa) brings about the well-known male or female physical characteristics. In cell makeup, females have two X chromosomes, while males have an X and a Y. The function of the short and stumpy Y chromosome in males is still mysterious. For some reason it triggers the development of maleness in the fetus. (The sex drive in both males *and* females, however, is related to the production of testosterone, not to chromosomal makeup.)

Various studies of the effect of hormones on animal behavior have been conducted. One of the earliest was done in 1849, by the German scientist Arnold Berthold, who discovered that roosters whose hormonal qualities were modified by castration stopped fighting, and lost interest in hens. More recent experiments with non-mammalian animals (for example, hens and cocks and toads) show that the injection of hormones can change behavior from male-type to female-type, and even completely change sex (for instance, in toads). In studies of mammals, similar results have emerged: for example, injection of androgen into female rhesus monkeys causes them to engage in "rough and tumble" play, and to mount other females, as if they were going to mate.

For obvious reasons, similar experiments with proper controls cannot be easily conducted on human beings. But no studies are necessary to document the clear differences on the physical level—in terms of hair and muscle growth, the ratio of muscle to fat, tallness, pelvic size, and other anatomical features. Some enterprising psychologists studied the book-carrying habits of students from elementary school to college, and concluded that males carry books more often by their side, while females tend to hug them to their chest with their arms. Mark Twain brings out additional behavioral differences in the novel, *Huckleberry Finn*: In one scene, Huck Finn is wearing a dress and trying to fool Mrs. Judith Loftus into thinking he is a girl. Mrs. Loftus suspects the impersonation and conducts her own tests, just to make sure. After watching him thread a needle, catch a piece of lead in his lap, and throw it at a rat, she exposes his deception, as Huck Finn tells it:

The woman kept looking at me pretty curious, and I didn't feel a bit comfortable. Pretty soon she says:

"What did you say your name was, honey?"

"M—Mary Williams" . . .

". . . What's your real name, now?"

"George Peters, mum."

"Well, try to remember it, George. Don't forget and tell me it's Elexander before you go, and then get out by saying it's George Elexander when I catch you. And don't go about women in that old calico. You do a girl tolerable poor, but you might fool men, maybe. Bless you, child, when you set out to thread a needle, don't hold the thread still and fetch the needle up to it; hold the needle still and poke the thread at it; that's the way a woman most always does, but a man always does t'other way. And when you throw at a rat or anything, hitch yourself up a-tiptoe and fetch your hand up over your head as awkward as you can, and miss your rat about six or seven foot. Throw stiff-armed from the shoulder, like there was a pivot there for it to turn on, like a girl; not from the wrist and elbow, with your arm out to one side, like a boy. And, mind you, when a girl tries to catch anything in her lap, she throws her knees apart; she don't clap them together, the way you did when you catched the lump of lead. Why I spotted you for a boy when you was threading the needle; and I contrived the other things just to make certain."

Whether Mark Twain or academic researchers have uncovered stereotypes or true sex-related behavioral characteristics, the characteristics in question are obviously on a superficial level. If there are psychological differences, however, our understanding of these differences would be more significant and important. And this is what we will be focusing on in what follows.

4.2 Psychological Differences

Gender ambiguities. As was mentioned above, the human fetus in the earliest stages is sexually undifferentiated. In most cases, a clear development of male or female physical characteristics takes place. But even in those cases, male *and* female hormones are present, and remnants of opposite-sex genitals and reproductive systems remain. Some types of biological anomalies bring out the ambiguities. Hermaphroditism, in which an individual is born with both male and female sexual systems, gives us a clear indication that sexual identity is just a matter of emphasis—no such thing as a "purely" masculine or feminine organism is to be found among humans, as well as among other animals. Personality characteristics such as homosexual or bisexual orientation give us even more concrete evidence of gender ambiguity. Plato in his dialogue, the *Symposium*, tried to make sense of this ambiguity by a creation myth: According to the account of one of the characters in the *Symposium*, the comedian-playwright Aristophanes, the gods created three types of humans—totally masculine, totally feminine, and a bisexual creature. But because the creatures got too powerful and ambitious, the gods "cut them down to size" literally, by dividing each type in half. A side effect of this action, besides weakening the power of humans, was that each type was now constantly searching for its "other half"—thus explaining homosexuality, lesbianism, and heterosexuality. Plato in a semi-humorous vein offered this story as a way to help explain the varied and sometimes anomalous type of sexual attraction found in humans.

More recently Carl Gustav Jung analyzed personality development in terms of androgyny, the psychological counterpart of physical bisexuality. According to Jung's theory, as discussed in Chapter 2, males typically tend to repress their female aspects, called the "anima" to the unconscious level; females, however, typically repress their male qualities, the "animus." Each sex then cannot deal directly with the specific unconscious image that they have formed, which tends to appear and reappear in their dreams. In conscious experience they can deal with the "anima" or "animus" only indirectly through "projection" on to members of the opposite sex. Some members of the opposite sex will better approximate the unconscious image that he or she will have; and this will help explain things like the varieties of romantic attraction that people feel (and answer questions like "what does she see in *him*?"). Jungian theory also tries to explain homosexuality and lesbianism with a similar approach: for various reasons, some males will tend to identify with a female persona and repress their animus, and some females will develop a consciously masculine persona and repress their anima. In such cases Jungian psychoanalysts may try to help patients become conscious of the repressed personae, or deal with individual or social conflicts that may be related to the course their personality development has taken.

Aside from one's acceptance or rejection of the Jungian psychotherapeutic approach, "androgyny" as an enhanced awareness of, and ability to empathize with, opposite-sex characteristics, is widely considered to be important for mature psychological development.

4.3 Historical Overview of Theories about M/F Differences

Following in Plato's footsteps, philosophers and psychologists, down through the ages, have tried to offer some viable generalizations to sum up what *appeared* to be a common-sense observation—that there *are* important and discernible differences between the sexes, over and above the more obvious physical differences.

Aristotle in his biological works came to the conclusion (just the opposite of the contemporary theory) that the default state of the human fetus is masculinity. But in about half of pregnancies, it happens, says Aristotle, that some fetuses do not arrive at full physical development, and these "incomplete" specimens turn out to be female! Aristotle's theory prevailed into the Middle Ages.

St. Thomas Aquinas, following the Aristotelean doctrine that a female was a *mas incompletum* (a male who during gestation had not attained to fetal maturity!) also accepted and promulgated Aristotle's psychological conclusion—that the incomplete development explained the fact that most women were deficient in the ability to reason, and were led by their emotions, instead of by rational considerations. It is not difficult to surmise the social and cultural ramifications that could be and were connected with the Aristotelian theory, which held sway for almost two thousand years.

Immanuel Kant (1724–1804) in one of his early works, *Observations on the Feeling of the Beautiful and the Sublime*, analyzed the differences between males and females in terms of differing *aesthetic* orientations. According to Kant, females generally have a special sense for, and appreciation of, the beautiful—objects, often small, or decorations, or works of art, characterized by qualities of beauty, such as tastefully applied colors, textures, tones, and so forth. Males, on the other hand, are less endowed with the ability to appreciate the beauty of small things, but have a special aptitude for the aesthetic appreciation of sublimity—objects or scenes or events which are large or grandiose, awe-inspiring, challenging the imagination—for example, massive mountain ranges, great historical events or individual feats of courage, and so on. Kant thought that women's aesthetic predilections also carried over into their approach to morality: they do not interpret morality in terms of rules and duties, as males most often do, but rather in the sense of tasteful and comely actions, performed in accord with "beautiful" virtues.

Søren Kierkegaard (1813–1855) is often classified as an "existentialist" because of his emphasis on individualism, which is a common existentialist theme. But Kierkegaard portrays male and female as illustrating almost two different types of individuals. Using terminology derived from the early nineteenth-century philosopher Hegel, Kierkegaard theorizes that men exist "for-themselves," while women exist "for-another." Such terminology in Hegelian philosophy does not have the connotations that we might attach to it. Existence-for-self is basically the quality of self-consciousness in humans; existence-for-another is interest in, and orientation to, others. There are both positives and negatives connected with these orientations. The personality-characteristic of existence-for-self can lead to heightened powers of reflection or to self-centeredness; the quality of existence-for-others can lead to altruism and social connectedness or to neurotic self-effacement.

According to Kierkegaard, women also have a different relationship to their own bodies than men. Women have a habitual sense of being in unity with their body, while men feel at a distance from their body, often at odds with it. Thus a Kierkegaardian might conclude that men are more likely than women to use and exploit their body to achieve goals like social or financial success, since their body takes on the aspect of an "instrument." Failure to listen to the body's "signals" may result in ulcers, heart attacks, or other problems. Empirical studies comparing differential male and female susceptibility to diseases may help to confirm this generalization.

Kierkegaard himself pointed to styles in art as a possible confirmation of his theory that there is an emphasis on body over "spirit" in females, but on spirit over the body in males. He observed that in paintings women are often depicted in sensuous repose (for example paintings of Venus sleeping), while males are typically portrayed in spirited action (such as paintings of Apollo or Zeus, never represented as sleeping). Kierkegaard's unscientific observation might be confirmed or disconfirmed by statistical analysis of artistic portraitures.

Karl Marx, as is well known, analyzed patterns of exploitation taking place in nineteenth-century capitalist systems. In his early philosophical works, he makes an interesting socio-political application of gender dynamics. According to Marx, the male attitude toward females offers us the best indication of their general attitude toward nature, the environment, society in general, and the lower classes in particular. If males take women as objects to be exploited, Marx argued, they tend to have the same attitude toward the environment, the lower classes, and so forth. Marx's solution was the inauguration of scientific socialism, or communism. Communism, unfortunately, was not spectacularly successful in eliminating female exploitation; but Marx's general observation about attitude patterns may be worth considering.

Psychologists in the twentieth century, as might be expected, have also been engaged in analysis of gender attributes. Sigmund Freud emphasized that no such thing as pure masculinity or pure femininity exists, although, due to biological and sociological factors, males generally tend to be more aggressive behaviorally and have a more intense sexual libido. Oswald Schwartz (1883–1949) following up on Freudian theories about sexuality, engaged in some philosophical speculation that bears comparisons with Kierkegaard's theory, mentioned above. Schwartz, however, focuses on the male/female relationship to the *external world* rather than the relationship to the body. He contends that women have a sense of being in unity with the external world, while in contrast men tend to feel separate from the world, and threatened by it, so that they need to disarm it, or dominate and control it. As a German psychologist, he also claimed to have the answer to a famous epistemological problem posed by the German philosopher, Kant (whose theory of gender was discussed above). According to Kant, in our knowledge of the external world, we are constantly making interconnections of sense data that we receive from objects, but we can never have any reliable knowledge of the way things *really* exist—we lack knowledge of the "things-in-themselves"—the objects or substances supposedly supporting the sense data that we perceive. But according to Schwartz, this is primarily a *male* problem, caused by the feeling of distance or alienation from the external world which males frequently have, but females seldom have. The result would be that many or most females, hearing about Kant's thing-in-itself problem, might be more likely than males to comment, "why would anyone have a problem like that?"

An extensive study of male and female characteristics was undertaken by the psychologists Catherine Miles and the pioneer in IQ testing, Lewis Terman, during the 1930s, and published in their book, *Sex and Personality*. Some of the main gender-based personality differences that emerged from their study are summarized on the following page.

Terman and Miles emphasize that many or all of these traits may be the result of cultural conditioning; they had no evidence that there are biological/genetic causes of the observed differences.

More recent studies have found some evidence for differential male-female math and language abilities. Psychologists Carol Travis and Carol Offir, for example, examined many of the claimed M/F differences in their 1977 book, *The Longest War: Sex Differences in Perspective*, and found that there appear to be some empirical grounds for asserting the sex *math/language* difference. Mathematical aptitude is closely correlated to visual-spatial abilities, for which boys tend to score higher in standardized tests than girls. The fact that in the sevenh grade fifty percent of the boys, and twenty-five percent of the girls score high in tests of spatial

Male traits	Female traits
(1) Adventuresomeness, which can take on various aspects—curiosity, exploration, willingness to gamble and take risks.	Conservatism, not in a political or religious sense, but more generally as cautiousness, unwillingness to take risks. An example/application might be the fact that it is often much less expensive to buy auto insurance for young women than young men, because of statistics on accidents and traffic citations for males under 25.
(2) Interest in success, as indicated by questionnaires given to boys about their future job or career objectives.	Interest in helping others, indicated by the fact that girls in career-choice questionnaires mentioned preference for altruistically-oriented careers—for example, nursing, social work—significantly more often than boys.
(3) Interest in things and events, indicated by topics of conversation among boys.	Interest in persons, indicated by typical conversations among girls.
(4) Aptitude in math, spatial ability, sense of direction, as evinced by standardized tests and school grades.	Language ability, indicated by grades and tests.
(5) "Objective" sexuality; sexual impulse often object-oriented, as indicated by prevalence of prostitution; and aroused by sight, as indicated by male interest in pornography.	"Subjective" sexuality; sexual impulse more closely connected with emotions and feelings—excited by touch

TABLE 4.1 Terman-Miles M/F Findings

visualization, combined with the biological "rules" for the inheritance of recessive characteristics from parents, suggests that this ability may be genetic; thus it is possible that the correlated mathematical aptitudes may be partly explained by genetics. Further recent evidence emerged from a Johns Hopkins study, in which it was found that when the mathematical portion of the Scholastic Aptitude test was administered to eighth graders with similar math preparation, half of the boys but not one of the girls scored above 600. Studies during the 1990s by David Lubinski and Camilla Benbow have corroborated the Terman/Miles conclusions about comparative math ability and about comparative male-female interest in things versus persons.

Tavris and Offir also note that the vast majority of tests indicate that girls definitely excel in verbal ability after age eleven, and that on tests of creativity which require verbal ability, girls typically score higher than boys. The differential M/F verbal ability may be conditioned in part by brain structure (see below), but may also have environmental explanations—for example, cultural influences leading girls to accomplish their goals by speech rather than in overtly aggressive ways.

We receive dramatic evidence that males are more *aggressive* than females from an examination of crime statistics and statistics about numbers and sex of prison inmates; only a small percentage of those incarcerated for violent crimes are female, and hardly any females are on death row. Likewise, standardized tests for aggression usually ascribe significantly higher scores for aggressivity to males than to females. However, it is not clear how much of this apparent aggressiveness is attributable to testosterone, androgen and the y-chromosome, and how much is attributable to cultural conditioning historically and worldwide. It is possible that females have been culturally conditioned to express an equal amount of aggression in subtle ways—verbally, or with "body language," or through "passive aggression" (retaliating against others through nonaction, or by subtly putting obstacles in their way).

Recent studies by developmental psychologists have indicated that there may be a significant difference in male and female approaches to *ethical decision-making*. Psychologist Lawrence Kohlberg devised a timetable of normal ethical development, based on a long-range study of male subjects. Kohlberg's schedule emphasized a gradual six-stage development to ethical decision-making on the basis of general principles, and claimed that his findings were applicable to both sexes. Carol Gilligan, however, basing her own research on controlled studies of the development of girls, claimed that mature female ethical development emphasizes consideration of contexts and personal relationships, instead of the application of abstract principles (this conclusion is similar to Kant's observations, cited above, about male and female ethical propensities).

Contemporary debate among psychologists on this issue has helped precipitate some divisions in the feminist movement (which has never been monolithic). Current divisions include "different voice" feminists, such as Deborah Tannen, Nel Noddings, and Gilligan herself, who emphasize female difference regarding ethics and values; "equal rights" or "equity" feminists, such as former Justice Ruth Bader Ginsburg, Camille Paglia, Elizabeth Fox-Genovese, Christina Hoff Sommers, and Katha Pollitt, emphasizing political and legal equalization of the status of women; and "radical" or "gender" feminists, including Andrea Dworkin, Gloria Steinem, Catharine MacKinnon, and others who focus on the need of female liberation from traditional subtle and overt male oppression. This latter group has criticized Carol Travis and other female psychologists for acceptance of theories about male superiority in mathematics, the differential male approach to sexuality, and so forth. Possibly in response to such criticisms, Carol Travis's more recent book, *The Mismeasure of Woman*, offers opinions regarding aggression, math ability, and other personality features which contradict opinions made in her earlier best-seller, *The Longest War*. Many feminists, not just the radicals, consider the provocative assertions about sex differences by sociobiologists (examples have already been given in Chapter 3) to be "bad science"—invalid extrapolations of data acquired from the study of animals or from theories about the "hunter-gatherer" stage of human evolution.

4.4 Some Socio-Political Considerations

The question about male/female differences is not just an academic question, but has political, social and ethical ramifications, as can be discerned from the above controversies. Most of the differences that do exist may be the result of a confluence of "nature" and "nurture" so tightly intertwined that it would be impossible to calculate with any precision the relative percentages of the contributions of heredity and environment. But *Dobzhansky's paradox*, discussed in the last chapter, can offer us one useful approach to the issue. Dobzhansky's observations about intermarriage are of course irrelevant in this case (unless we consider lesbianism as an attempt to maintain a superior female caste!); but his theory about the effect of social mobility on the status quo of classes appears quite relevant to the issue of M/F equality. As John Stuart Mill argued eloquently and at great length in Chapter 1 of his 1868 essay, *On the Subjection of Women*, we can have no clear knowledge of the general capabilities of males *or* females unless and until maximum environmental opportunities have been presented for a sufficient span of time. For example, as some have suggested, *math ability in females* might increase to parity with males in single-sex education environments, or when a sufficient number of female math teachers and professors supply role models; *lesser aggression of females* might become a thing of the past, as aggressive activities become less a matter of physical strength, and more a matter of technological superiority; *verbal ability among males* might flourish in environments in which the use of physical strength to attain objectives is disvalued, or fathers begin talking to their sons as much as mothers to their daughters.

In principle, even the provocative assertions of sociobiologists could be verified or disproven, given enough time and considerable changes in possibilities of social mobility. Some have pointed to the Israeli *kibbutzim* social experiment as confirmation of the fact that M/F differences are biologically based, and cannot be changed by social conditioning. The kibbutz movement began in the early part of the twentieth century in Palestine, and consisted of founding largely agricultural communities in which absolute social equality was the keynote. The founders of the kibbutzim were actually implementing a plan similar to one proposed by Plato thousands of years ago, and also fantasized by some utopian theorists, like St. Thomas More (in *Utopia*)—developing a community (kibbutz) in which everything would be held in common, tasks would be distributed equally without considerations of gender or social status, and children would be raised in common instead of in nuclear families. With the advent of the state of Israel in 1948 hundreds of *kibbutzim* were established. But the initial ideals have been gradually modified, apparently because of free choices on the part of the inhabitants. Private property and even entrepreneurship has largely replaced the ideal of communal ownership, most children are raised in their own family, child care and domestic work are largely assigned to women, while leadership roles and heavy labor/technical tasks are generally allotted to men. This experiment is admittedly not definitive, since it was conducted with only a small population (three percent of the Israeli population) and consisted of volunteers deeply steeped in religious and ethnic traditions. Much more data from other religious and ethnic groups would be required, and on a much larger scale, to offer more convincing confirmation or refutation of the sociobiological assertions.

4.5 Possible Implications of M/F Brain Differentials

The chart that follows, covering just a few variables connected with male and female hemispheres of the brain, will give some indication of how much more complex the scientific data are to analyze in the case of human gender differences, than in the case (discussed in Chapter 3) of the drosophila fruit fly! The chart focuses primarily on the connection of verbal and spatial and visual abilities with the biological differences prevailing in male and female brains.

According to Simon Baron-Cohen in *The Essential Difference*, some fundamental behavioral/personality differences can be traced to this differential cerebral structure. It is commonly pointed out that the dominance of the right hemisphere of the brain in most males can offer advantages in regard to spatial and visual abilities, and indirectly in regard to mathematical abilities; while the faster development of the left hemisphere in females, along with the distinctive female ability to share some left hemisphere tasks with the right hemisphere, can offer advantages in language ability. But Baron-Cohen claims that the differences that can be traced to male and female brain structure, and are substantiated by numerous psychological tests, are more fundamental than this. In males, there seems to be a biological/neurological basis for *systemizing*. This involves the ability to trace causes, make judgments about input and output, figure out series, and abstract from environmental distractions, including persons. Female brain structure, on the other hand, seems to contribute to the ability to *empathize*. As noted in the Terman-Miles studies mentioned above, and other studies, girls, even from the earliest ages, excel in empathy; their interests and conversations are oriented towards persons, they pick up attitudes and emotional states of others more accurately, and tend to choose person-oriented jobs and careers. Systemizing is probably associated with the greater ability in math noted in males, and empathizing ability is probably conducive to the greater facility in language noted in females.

The chart below may also bring out the fact that factors which never come into consideration with discussions of gender—such as right- or left-handedness, or the rate of cerebral development— might be relevant to the issue of gender differences. And one possible paradoxical conclusion might emerge from considering the gender characteristics that may be connected with the structure of the male and female brain: If males, along with the greater *lateralization* of the two hemispheres of their brain, tend to systemize and analyze more than females, the tendency to systematically differentiate the two sexes may be a predominantly male characteristic. If females, in tandem with their greater *communication between* the two hemispheres of their brain, are more prone to empathize than males—and to empathize *with* males—the tendency to downplay the differences between the sexes may be a typically female characteristic. If this is so, the very process of finding differences in

Left Hemisphere Development (primary center for language proficiency)	Right-Left *Coordination* between the two hemispheres of the brain (generally greater in females).	Right Hemisphere Development (regulates spatial and visual abilities; also music)
Develops more quickly in females	Females, especially right-handed females, are more likely to have verbal and spatial capacities located in *both* hemispheres of the brain	Dominant in males, especially right-handed males, in whom the right hemisphere develops more rapidly
Right-handed males are more likely to have their speech-center on the left than left-handed males	In both right- and left-handed females, a lesser degree of brain specialization exists; thus, after a stroke on the left side of the brain, women show much less severe loss of speech than men	In girls, the right hemisphere develops more slowly than in boys
Greater lateralization (i.e., separation, lack of connection, between the two hemispheres) in males may be correlated with less natural language ability as a function of the left hemisphere.	The male brain is laterally differentiated and highly structured, as compared with the female brain, which is more symmetrically organized and less tightly structured (women can shift more easily between the two hemispheres, and combine the functions of the right and left side of the brain more effectively than men).	
Right-handed girls develop the left hemisphere more rapidly than left-handed girls		

TABLE 4.2 Male-Female Brain Development

the sexes may be a primordial male tendency, while females tend more toward gender integration! However, no systematic studies of *this* hypothetical difference are available to give us direction at present.

5

The Future of Human Evolution

The human race has always been in progress toward the better and will continue to be so henceforth. To him who does not consider what happens in just some one nation but also has regard to the whole scope of all the peoples on earth who will gradually come to participate in progress, this reveals the prospect of an immeasurable time—provided at least that there does not, by some chance, occur a second epoch of natural revolution which will push aside the human race to clear the stage for other creatures. . . . Gradually violence on the part of the powers will diminish and obedience to the laws will increase. There will arise in the body politic perhaps more charity and less strife in lawsuits, more reliability in keeping one's word, etc., partly out of love of honor, partly out of well-understood self-interest. And eventually this will also extend to nations in their external relations toward one another up to the realization of the cosmopolitan society, without the moral foundation in mankind having to be enlarged in the least; for that, a kind of new creation (supernatural influence) would be necessary.

—IMMANUEL KANT, *An Old Question Raised Again: Is the Human Race Constantly Progressing?*

A new anthropological space, the *knowledge space*, is being formed today, which could easily take precedence over the spaces of earth, territory, and commerce that preceded it. . . . The most socially useful goal will no doubt be to supply ourselves with the instruments for sharing our mental abilities in the construction of collective intellect or imagination. Internet-worked data would then provide the technical infrastructure for the collective brain or *hypercortex* of living communities.

—Pierre Lévy, "Collective Intelligence"

It would not be an exaggeration to say that in the modern Western world, evolution for scientists is not just a theory, but an all-pervasive world view. The theory of evolution in the strict, original sense applies to the biological development of various plant and animal species, including humans. But some theorists have extrapolated biological evolution into social and cultural evolution, even considering possible future evolutionary patterns. Likewise, physicists and cosmologists have applied the evolutionary perspective to the cosmos as a whole, theorizing about what sort of "chance developments" took place after the "Big Bang," leading into the "evolution" of the first elements, then the galaxies, and our own galaxy and planetary system. Some cosmologists even theorize about an evolution of multiple universes, leading eventually to our own special universe. Thus, at least for some scientists, the evolution of the "tree of life" is just one branch of the ongoing evolutions which supply the ultimate horizons of our knowledge.

But the general public, according to a recent National Science survey, has not fully accepted the idea of biological evolution, let alone evolution in the cosmological sense. According to a 1999 National Science Board survey, fifty-six percent of those questioned did not know, or did not believe, that "humans developed from earlier species of animals." In six Gallup polls about evolution taken from 1982 to 2004, consistently only a small minority (9–12 percent) believed in evolution as a purely natural phenomenon, without any divine guidance. For some people, the idea just seems preposterous that humans could have been derived from reptiles, fish, and other species; for others, seeing an apparent contradiction with the account of creation in the Bible, the theory of evolution is rejected on religious grounds. Thus according to a March 2000 poll cited in the *New York Times*, the majority of those consulted wanted *both* evolution and creationism to be taught in the public schools. This sounds contradictory. But perhaps not, depending on what is meant by "creationism."

Some scientists, with a strong belief in the power of chance developments through "natural selection," view Charles Darwin's theory of evolution as a substitute for the idea of creation by God; others consider it possible that God could have created the world and the human race through an evolutionary process. Thus, the Jewish physicist Gerald Schroeder, in *Genesis and the Big Bang*, argues that the account of the "days" of creation in the first book of the Bible is compatible with the theory of special relativity because of the warping and compression of time at the very beginning; physicists Robert Jastrow in *God and the Astronomers* and Paul Davies in *God and the New Physics* discuss the strong evidence for intentional design rather than mere chance in the evolution of the universe; and the biologist Kenneth Miller in *Finding Darwin's God* argues that theism and Darwinist "natural selection" are completely compatible. But other biologists, accepting evolution in general, claim that there are gaps in the Darwinian theory. Michael Behe in *Darwin's Black Box* maintained that the development of initial molecular complexity in organisms is unexplainable by natural selection, and defended "intelligent design" in the 2005 *Kitzmiller v. Dover* trial in Harrisburg, Pennsylvania, concerning the teaching of Darwinian evolution in public schools.

Likewise many scientists, including the late Stephen Jay Gould, a Harvard paleontologist and no friend of creationists, have pointed out that the rapid global appearance of new phyla about a half billion years ago (the Cambrian period) is an explosion without any pre-Cambrian fossils of chordates, arthropods, and other phyla. Some critics consider this to be a fatal flaw in Darwinism; but Gould and other scientists committed to Darwinist theory say this is merely an energizing challenge for modern science: the fossils must be there, enterprising scientists will discover them, or discover the reason they are not there. Still other scientists, proponents of "intelligent design" as well as creationists, view the lack of evidence for developments after the appearance of *Homo sapiens* on the evolutionary "tree" to be a significant and insufficiently recognized weakness in Darwinian theory.

For many of the critics, the problem is not evolution itself, but "natural selection." Darwinian "natural selection" depends on billions of chance developments to explain not only developments within species (microevolution) but also transitions between species (macroevolution). Natural selection is an explanation focusing on the reproductive capacities of species, means of defense from predators, presence or absence of food supplies and a livable climate, presence or absence of catastrophes such as meteorite collisions, and so forth; such an approach does away with considerations of teleology—any intentional design or purposefulness—in favor of purely mechanical explanations. A contemporary of Darwin, Alfred Russel Wallace, recognized by Darwin as a co-discoverer of evolution, interpreted the evolutionary developments from a teleological perspective. Others besides Wallace have also offered teleological explanations.

5.1 Social and Cultural Evolution

Leaving behind the controversies, which are rife, regarding *physical* evolution, our primary concern in what follows is with theories of social and cultural evolution. Fortunately, these theories are not necessarily affected by any defects that may exist in the theory of physical evolution—theories of social/cultural evolution stand or fall on the basis of whether they help us to understand or interpret human life. Someone who did not believe in physical evolution could without contradiction believe in the progressive evolution of society or in certain predictable stages for the unfolding of civilization. Examples of pre-Darwinian, classical, theories of social evolution include the *City of God*, written by St. Augustine in the fourth century, which traces the stages of development of the conflicting human and divine kingdoms in history; *The New Science* of Giambattista Vico (1668–1774), who analyzes the development of humankind from stages of myth to rationality and modern science; and Kant's *Idea of a Universal History*, which sketches a very optimistic scenario of inevitable human progress. G.W.F. Hegel, like Kant, did not believe in the physical evolution of humans from lower forms, but is noted for elaborating a theory of the historical evolution of humans toward greater freedom in his posthumously published *Lectures on the Philosophy of History*.

Post-Darwinian theories of social evolution have also proliferated since the end of the nineteenth century. The evolutionist Thomas Huxley (1825–1895) maintained that human evolution did not exactly follow the Darwinian "script" of the lower species, which involved "survival of the fittest" after various conflicts for resources; but the higher stages could proceed in a more rational fashion without the rather brutal struggle for survival that characterizes the other species. Karl Marx, attending London lectures by Huxley on evolution, was strongly influenced by Huxley's theory of social evolution, and also by Hegel's philosophy of history and the economic theory of Adam Smith (1723–1790). Combining a methodology of "Hegelian dialectic" with Smith's political-economic observations on the progress of capitalism, Marx developed a theory of "scientific socialism" which predicted that capitalism, built on selfishness, would eventually require greater and greater co-operation among industries and labor forces—evolving into communism, and a new type of non-selfish consciousness.

Other theorists moved in a quite different direction than Marx. Herbert Spencer (1820–1903) in his *Principles of Sociology* hypothesized continual development toward greater complexity (and hence greater intelligence). Oswald Spengler (1880–1936) in *The Decline of the West* hypothesized that the various cultures go through life-cycles of flourishing and decline; he thought contemporary civilization was heading for a world empire under the control of Germany. Friedrich Nietzsche (1844–1900) in his *Will to Power* and other works, spoke about an upward, *non-*Darwinian thrust of evolution to produce quality instead of quantity, that is, at least one *Übermensch* ("superman"), or at least someone approximating to a superman. By "superman" (male gender intended), Nietzsche meant one individual who fully epitomizes the "Will to Power" supposedly prevailing in all biological evolution. Nietzsche even developed a rather esoteric "qualifying" test to determine if and when the *Übermensch* had arrived: this superior being would be an individual so fully conscious of, and committed to, the creative power manifested in the evolution of life, that he could will an eternal recurrence over and over again of everything that has happened just as it has happened!

Such theories are examples of diverse attempts to get at the "big picture" regarding human evolution. Whatever one may think of them, they at least bring major questions into the limelight: Are there *patterns* to be discerned in the past? If so, perhaps we can extrapolate these same patterns predictively into the future. In particular, we might be able to determine whether future development will move in the direction of greater *individualization* or *collectivity*. This issue is uppermost in the writings of the theorists we will now consider.

5.2 Patterns in the Past

(1) The stage of *primitive co-consciousness.* According to psychologist Julian Jaynes, those who lived in the ancient world had a very different mentality than moderns. If we examine the earliest writings, which date from around 3000 B.C., to examine their development, we see that they had a mind split into two segments, a "bicameral mind." For example, the voices and visions that Abraham and Moses and others in the ancient world frequently heard were due to a kind of benign schizophrenia. Their minds were split into a "God" part, and a "man" part. Instead of making plans and decisions for life, which we expect of adults in the modern world, the major plans and decisions in the ancient world were attributed to divinities. Great leaders and heroes had their initiatives authorized and supported by God or the gods. This kind of authorization was necessary because primitive human beings had no concept of things modern civilization takes for granted—personality, individuality, personal liberty and responsibility. If we examine ancient literatures, we find that signs of individuality are almost completely lacking in the ancient world until about 1000 B.C., when we find indications in poets and philosophers that human development is beginning to include the concept of a personal "inner space." Plato, Aristotle and other philosophers, especially when they focused on the operations of the mind and decision-making, were forerunners in this development, which continued in more advanced ways into the middle ages.

What evidence do we have for Jaynes's contention? The existence of slavery into the modern era may be a case in point. Are we to suppose that the vast majority of people up to the seventeenth century were naively ignorant of the evils of slavery, or so immoral that they didn't care? Isn't it more likely that most of them in that era had no notion of the dignity of each individual and the inalienable individual rights that are connected with this? In modern Western societies, we consider slavery to be immoral and, if we are Christians, we consider it un-Christian. But in the canonical Christian Scriptures St. Paul advises slaves to be obedient to their masters and in his epistle, *Philemon*, even urges a slave master to receive his newly converted runaway slave back without punishing him. Major moral philosophers up to the beginning of the nineteenth century accepted slavery as an institution, although they sometimes recommended restrictions—for example, only allowing prisoners of war to be enslaved. Thus the common abhorrence of slavery in modern civilized societies appears to be an offshoot of a change in consciousness concerning the value of the individual.

Other psychologists also emphasize the significant difference between ancient and modern perspectives. According to Carl Gustav Jung, primitive peoples did not make the distinction between subject and object that we take for granted. We talk about the "psychic" or "subjective" as something internal, separate from what is "out there" and "physical"; but our distant ancestors made no such sharp distinctions. They found psychic elements in plants and animals, resulting in an animistic view of the world, and leading to the creation of idols and divinities in the world. Oswald Schwartz maintains that the ancients did not make the distinctions we make between dream and reality, between symbols and the objects that they signify. Hostile forces that appear in dreams are taken as realities that must be conquered, and injury to the totem of a tribe is taken as injury to the tribe itself. Likewise, they did not develop procedures to connect distinct causes with their effects, which is so essential to modern science. Instead of trying to trace diseases to their actual specific causes, as in modern Western medicine, they interpreted them as bad omens or punishments from the gods for some act or omission.

(2) The stage of *individualization*. According to the cultural anthropologist Claude Lévi-Strauss, the modern world (from the sixteenth century to the present) marks the transition from "nature" to "culture." That is, modern people are no longer highly involved with the cycles of nature and relationships to nat-

ural kinship groups; they view their individual consciousness as separate from the world and other people. Daniel Defoe's novel, *Robinson Crusoe* serves as an apt illustration of this mentality—the resourceful person, on his own, left to his own devices, separate from the rest of the world but trying to take advantage of it as much as possible. The positive aspects, almost the philosophy, of individualism are championed by the nineteenth-century essayist, Henry Thoreau in *Walden, or, Life in the Woods.* In the twentieth century the cult of individualism has sometimes been carried to an extreme—exemplified by references to the "me" generation and by books like *Looking Out for #1, Winning through Intimidation, Pulling Your Own Strings,* and many similar titles.

The processes of individualization are most pronounced in the industrialized Western world. Differences in consciousness can have political and cultural ramifications. Westerners may tend to look down on other cultures as overemphasizing communal structures and slow to appreciate individuality, and thus resistant to recognition of individual rights and democratic ideals. But people in all parts of the world may be caught up in various stages of social evolution. An understanding of the movement toward personalization which has taken place in a large part of the world can help us to understand and interpret past developments. For example, it becomes clear why very little attention is given to the concept of personality and individuality in ancient literature and philosophy, and hardly any explicit discussion of individual rights, the possibility of free choice, and the like—which are significant topics in contemporary philosophy.

5.3 Projections of the Future

(3) *A third stage?* Scientists tell us that, barring a nuclear disaster or a cosmic catastrophe, the planet Earth will be habitable for at least another two billion years; thus, if the human species survives along with the earth, there will be approximately one hundred million generations to follow the present generation. If this is true, we are now situated at the very beginning of social and cultural evolution, as the "embryonic" stage in a long process; and we

might wonder, are things going to continue as usual? Are any higher stages of the evolution of human consciousness possible? And if they are possible, can we *know* anything about them?

This is a question about the future. Scientists are not ordinarily occupied with predicting the future, but they can and do make predictions, with varying degrees of accuracy—and not just the "iffy" predictions about weather by meteorologists. Physicists will project with great accuracy the trajectories of missiles and the paths of satellites or space probes; biologists and ecologists make predictions, which are not always listened to by authorities, about the depletion of the rain forests, the thinning out of the ozone layer and "global warming"; and political scientists, except in very close elections, can give us fairly reliable predictions of the outcome of an election after only a small sampling of the vote in selected key districts is tabulated. Can social evolutionists make predictions with any reliability? Some have tried:

Karl Marx, who was mentioned above as a post-Darwinian theorist of social evolution, predicted that post-capitalist socio-economic relations would result in a new type of human being, "communist man [and woman]" with a qualitatively different type of consciousness. Since selfishness, depravity, crime, oppression and manipulation are results of capitalist economic relations, the replacement of capitalism with scientific socialism, according to Marx, would result in a new type of consciousness, unselfish, cooperative, no longer prone to crime and corruption.

The Canadian electronic media expert, Marshall McLuhan, in his 1964 best-seller, *Understanding Media*, studied the transition from print media (such as newspapers and books) which accent individual consciousness, to the electronic media (especially television), which orient people toward a "global village" mentality. He predicted that just as Gutenberg's invention of printing had paved the way for the modern individualistic type of consciousness, so also the new media would bring about a return to primitive oral traditions, but on a global scale. People sitting in a library or a reading room with their heads buried in books or newspapers have to shut out the rest of the world, by the very nature of their concentration; but people sitting in a living room or lounge watching television have a quite different type of experience, communal in its emphasis, even if no one else is watching with them. Some examples of what McLuhan had in mind would be major worldwide cable and satellite TV transmissions of major events such as the Olympic Games, and global televised distribution of movies, sitcoms, and quiz shows. McLuhan thought that as such global media experiences happen more and more, people around the world will get to the point where they no longer consider themselves separate peoples, but just one "global village." (International network and cable transmissions by "embedded" reporters of the 2003 U.S. invasion of Iraq are probably not the sort of unifying experiences that McLuhan had in mind).

In a more spiritual vein, Sri Aurobindo Ghose, originally an Indian activist for independence from Britain, who later devoted himself to yogic contemplation and the study of evolution, theorized that the evolution of the earth had taken place in three stages: matter, life, and mind, and that what remains for the future is the evolution from mind to Supermind. This latter, ongoing evolution would take place in successive stages: the recognition of the Divine within consciousness, the expansion of consciousness through a higher light to embrace the Divine in the "All," and finally the descent of Supermind into the consciousness of one and all. The total progress of evolution of the earth and evolution of mind is depicted in concentric expanding circles in the accompanying diagram on the following page.

A less mystical but no less speculative theory was proposed by Lewis Thomas, a biologist, physician, and director of the Sloan Kettering Institute for cancer research. In his book, *The Lives of a Cell*, and other works, he predicted that the examples of cellular coordination that we see in coral reefs are indicators of the sort of advanced developments of life that will take place in human beings. In other words, since the distinctive thing about human life is the power of thought, we are evolving after the pattern of coral reefs into shoals of thought, reefs of thought, which transcend the individual and develop into superstructures in which individuals will participate.

The most highly structured theory of social and cultural evolution, however, was developed by the French Jesuit priest and

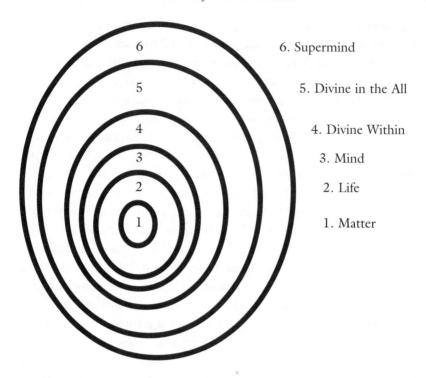

6. Supermind

5. Divine in the All

4. Divine Within

3. Mind

2. Life

1. Matter

FIGURE 5.1 Sri Aurobindo's Theory

paleontologist Pierre Teilhard de Chardin (1881–1955). Most of Teilhard's writings were published posthumously, since he was prohibited by his Jesuit superiors from publishing his views during his lifetime because of theological misgivings. In these books and articles, he elaborates on the future as well as the past, in great detail. In his book, *The Human Phenomenon*, he argues that ordinary physical energy, "tangential energy," cannot account for the development of higher species in evolution, no matter how gradual the development may be. In order to explain the tendency of evolution to produce more complex organisms, with higher and more unified types of consciousness, we have to presuppose a different type of energy, "radial energy," in addition to tangential energy. This latter type of energy is leading teleologically to an ultimate state, which paradoxically combines supreme complexity with the highest possible state of unity. As mankind evolves toward this ultimate state, it will arrive at a state of "communal consciousness" which will cover the earth and be participated in by all individual humans. This will be the third stage of evolution, going beyond the state of primitive co-consciousness and also beyond the present state which emphasizes individual consciousness.

Teilhard's third stage sounds like some of the other models we have considered above, including those of Marx and Sri Aurobindo. But it differs from these others in some important respects. Although Teilhard uses the term, "collective consciousness," to describe the third stage, it is a paradoxical type of collectivism, an anti-collectivistic collectivism, in which individuality is not submerged but instead enhanced and accentuated. Teilhard criticised collectivistic theories like communism which tended to subordinate or extinguish individuality to arrive at collective unity. He pointed out a basic principle applicable to all evolution—"unity diversifies." As applied to biological evolution, this means that all the higher stages of unity in living things are also higher stages of organic diversity—for example, primates like chimpanzees are more diversified in their organs and abilities than lower species, but also have a correspondingly greater ability to unify these diverse capabilities. But the same principle also applies to socio-cultural development, and this, according to Teilhard, is where the communists made serious mistakes. They did not realize that any great increase in the social unity of human beings would also require a parallel increase in diversity and individuality, in order to qualify as a truly organic step forward. Teilhard characterizes the communists as the "Neanderthals of the third stage [of cultural evolution]"—an important transitional group, since they emphasize the move to greater communality, but deficient in the simplistic methods they chose to arrive at that state.

Teilhard offers some analogies to explain how unity and diversity go hand-in-hand: If we have a close relationship to a friend, we find that our union with this friend enhances our individuality instead of submerging or compromising it. In fact, this is a sign that we are involved in a true friendship. Or, if we are involved in a tightly-knit group for some purpose, our identification with the goals of the group likewise enhances rather than diminishes our sense of individuality. Finally, if we have ever had a mystical/religious experience, the sense we have of being united with the Absolute or a higher Being in no way subtracts from our personal identity, but increases our awareness of it.

5.4 Contemporary Harbingers of a Third Stage

According to Teilhard, if we analyze the situation of the contemporary world, we find some major diversifying and unifying factors that, if properly co-ordinated, may presage the coming of a new stage of social consciousness for mankind. The *diversifying factors* include the tremendous development of private enterprise and "fluid money" (investment capital, etc.) in the economic sphere, and the widespread development of the awareness of individual liberty and responsibility in the political sphere. An additional diversifying factor is the "knowledge explosion," combined with the extraordinary advances in information-technology systems, which increases the possibilities of access to information for everyone, with a corresponding multiplication of the individual's power of choice. But at the same time, important and unprecedented *unifying factors* have also emerged in the contemporary world. The concept of space-time, which has become our common paradigm in tandem with Einstein's theory of special relativity, is not just a scientific breakthrough but is gradually affecting our world view, so that we are beginning to see our particular geographical and temporal situation in the larger context of an ongoing spiral towards unification with other evolving areas, and we are beginning to evolve intentionally, with possibilities for evolutionary control, instead of experiencing evolution as something that "happens to us."

Ironically, even the two World Wars in the twentieth century, which drew Europeans and English-speaking countries together to combat dictatorial regimes, have led to the creation of organizations to maintain unity and perpetuate peace—the United Nations, NATO, and subsequent economic and political alliances. More obvious to most people are the advances in communication and transportation, which allow us in the twenty-first century to communicate instantly with persons in all parts of the world, and go to any place in the world in a matter of hours. Electronics and information technology, mentioned above as a diversifying factor, can also paradoxically be a unifying factor, especially in view of the worldwide spread of internet communication. The French "hypermedia" specialist, Pierre Lévy, using Teilhardian language, theorizes that current developments in cyberspace technology are producing a literal "meeting of the minds" and developing a "collective intelligence" through a collective brain or *hypercortex* of living communities.

Teilhard observes that in all of evolution, physical as well as social and cultural, a key factor has been the "critical threshold"— a state at which changes rise to a state of supreme tension, giving rise to a breakthrough to some new stage. For example, in physical evolution, major leaps to higher species were apparently brought about by crises such as the scarcity of food resources, the harshness of the climate, meteorite collisions, and so forth. In the evolution of human consciousness, we may also be close to critical thresholds which may require an advance to a higher state, in order to avoid dire consequences. For example, the very real present possibility of a nuclear holocaust extinguishing entire nations, or even all life as we know it, due to an accidental firing of missiles, or aggression from a hostile nuclear power, may, in the best of scenarios, lead us to form permanent institutions for nuclear disarmament and peace. The buildup of pollution, as a side-effect of industry and technology, is a threat to life, and may possibly lead to worldwide ecological cooperation. The astronomical financial deficits affecting the U.S. and many other countries, may lead indirectly to more effective geoeconomic co-operation, in order to avoid catastrophic situations in future generations. All such developments contribute to great tension; but possibly the sort of tension which will be the springboard to a higher level of consciousness.

Teilhard's projected result of these developments is a new type of consciousness, in which earth's inhabitants are *literally* "thinking as one world." He envisions a globe covered with a "noosphere"—myriads of grains of thought forming a collective consciousness. The social and political characteristics of this consciousness would be simultaneously greater individualization *and* greater communitarianism. If we would look for signs of the development of this next stage, we would do best to search for paradoxical unities-in-diversity—social entities which at one and the same time indicate enhanced diversity and higher unities. Some examples from contemporary developments might include the European Common Market, now united economically through a unified currency (the *Euro*); various European movements contemplating a possible federal government formed out of extremely diverse national cultures; and internet and satellite communications offering a seamless band of communication circling almost all parts of the globe.

But a "reality check" is in order. We should not misunderstand what Teilhard is suggesting. He is not hypothesizing a higher type of organization, but a higher *organism*, a new level of human life, in which each individual will maintain his or her individuality and privacy to the maximum, but also be in intimate organic communion with all other consciousness. This is admittedly hard to imagine, but Teilhard argues that this is where the "trajectory of evolution" appears to be heading. Just as a physicist, knowing all the variables, such as the initial speed and angle of a missile and the wind resistance, can predict where the missile will land, so also an evolutionist like Teilhard, knowing the patterns of co-ordination of complexity and consciousness in the whole of evolution, may be able to predict the eventual emergence of some higher stage of complexity/consciousness.

Looking around us, we may still seem far removed from the highly speculative vision of unity-in-difference envisaged by Teilhard. But, like utopian ideas from the past and modern science-fiction literature, it may inspire improvements, and even be predictive of what is to come. Much that was science fiction just a few decades ago has now become reality. Skeptics about any emerging unification of civilization will point out the undeniable diversification and balkanization taking place in the world; but from Teilhard's perspective precisely such phenomena could be taken as signs of humanity's evolution into a super-organism, since "unity *diversifies*."

6

Is Human Nature a Unity or a Duality?

Is there any principle in all nature more mysterious than the union of soul with body; by which a supposed spiritual substance acquires such an influence over a material one, that the most refined thought is able to actuate the grossest matter? Were we empowered, by a secret wish, to remove mountains, or control the planets in their orbit; this extensive authority would not be more extraordinary, nor more beyond our comprehension.

—DAVID HUME, *An Enquiry Concerning Human Understanding* 7:1

Mental and physical events are, on all hands, admitted to present the strongest contrast in the entire field of being. The chasm which yawns between them is less easily bridged over by the mind than any interval we know. Why, then, not call it an absolute chasm, and say not only that the two worlds are different, but that they are independent? . . . I have heard a most intelligent biologist say: 'It is high time for scientific men to protest against the recognition of any such thing as consciousness in a scientific investigation' . . . It is to my mind quite inconceivable that consciousness should have *nothing to do* with a business which it so faithfully attends. And the question, 'What has it to do?' is one which psychology has no right to 'surmount,' for it is her plain duty to consider it.

—WILLIAM JAMES, *Psychology*

It seems clear that humans have arrived at what was characterized in the last chapter as the "second stage" of social/cultural evolution—the stage characterized by a consciousness of individuality. But is individual human personality a *duality* in which a mind or soul can be really distinguished from body and brain; or a unitary organism in which operations like thinking or remembering or imagining are just phenomenal aspects not really distinct from the organism in which they appear? Examination of our personal experiences can give us an indication of how this question arises, and why a problem of interpretation exists.

6.1 Experiential Aspects

(1) *Experiential grounds for belief in the unity of human personality.* Both positive and negative emotions offer us evidence of personal *unity*. If we are in a psychological state of joy or elation, and someone asks us whether this experience is physical or mental, the question would be irrelevant, since it is obviously both. In times of joy pleasurable feelings pervade our body, leading us to laugh or cry, often to speak or act; but we are also in an enhanced mental state, which increases our self-consciousness and impresses itself on our memory. Negative emotions are similarly ambiguous; fear, shame, guilt and anxiety are not only in the mind, but are even to a certain extent physically measurable. This is indicated by the use of lie detectors by FBI personnel and professional polygraphers. Although lie-detector tests are not routinely admissible as evidence in criminal and civil trials, advanced polygraph apparatus, measuring changes in blood pressure, heart beat, color of complexion, brain waves, and galvanic skin response can offer information about the state of mind of most subjects, with a probability that far exceeds chance. In many cases, when people lie, *something* happens to them physically. Our common experience also shows us that when we are intensely angry we notice gastric changes and suffer from sleeplessness; and our changes in pulse and blood pressure during such experiences are often measurable; but in addition to these physical changes, we also have thoughts of revenge, retaliation, or what we can do to save our reputation, etc. In other

words, no clear line between what is physical and what is mental is evident in such experiences.

(2) *Experiential grounds for belief in the duality of human personality.* The experience of personal *duality* is typically in the form of a causal relationship, either of the body affecting the mind or of the mind affecting the body.

Body→mind interactions are cases in which some bodily condition is influential in bringing about a mental or psychological state. We know, for instance, that food, drugs and physical exercise can affect our mental state for better or worse. Menstruation in some women brings about a cluster of symptoms (PMS) which sometimes includes psychological disturbances such as depression or anxiety; likewise, hypoglycemia (low blood sugar) is associated in some persons with depression and/or feelings of fear or hysteria. In 1916–1927, a viral sleeping sickness outbreak, from which patients initially recovered, eventually triggered severe mental symptoms (catatonia). The briefly successful attempt to help these patients was dramatized in the movie, *Awakenings.* Such examples appear to strengthen our conviction that bodily conditions can have an effect on the mind.

Mind→body interactions offer us the opposite type of example. In such cases, a mental attitude or belief appears to bring about a physical condition. Therapists often counsel their clients to focus on pleasant thoughts to help with blood pressure problems or other physical conditions. One of the best-known examples of the effect of mind on body is the use of placebos in the testing of drugs. Subjects are typically divided up into a group to which a new drug is being administered, and a "control" group, with similar symptoms or needs, but receiving pills, tablets, injections, etc. which have no medicinal value. Often improvements or even cures take place in the control group, apparently from the belief that they were receiving an effective medication. In the treatment of warts, especially in young patients, various versions of the physician's *Merck Manual* advise using "suggestions" with no medicinal value, such as painting the warts with gentian violet, focusing light or heat on them, even "hexing"; and in one experiment, adult patients were successfully hypnotized to make all the warts on one side of their body disappear, while the warts on the other side remained. Such examples provide us with evidence that the mind as a cause, presumably distinct from the body, can have an effect on physical health.

6.2 Positions Taken in the History of Philosophy

Philosophers down through the ages have tried to explain these apparently contradictory types of experiences. Their analyses have led to two diametrically opposed interpretations:

(1) *Monism* emphasizes the unity of the human psyche. This approach is quite often "reductionistic," that is, it attempts to reduce experiences that are apparently mental to something physical, *or* experiences that are apparently physical to something mental—thus involving a reinterpretation. We will consider the extreme versions of monism.

Extreme materialistic monists find the distinction of physical from mental unacceptable—a "Humpty Dumpty" syndrome which breaks up the human psyche and then encounters all sorts of pseudo-problems resulting from the unnecessary breakup. The ancient Greek atomists Democritus (460–370 B.C.) and Epicurus (341–270 B.C.) argued that all things, including mental phenomena, are merely the result of the movements and interactions of invisible atoms; even "soul" was just a special type of atom, and could not survive apart from the body. Contemporary materialists rely not only on modern atomic theory but also on neurophysiology and other scientific disciplines, either to reduce cognitive operations to activities centered in the brain, or to offer "behavioral" accounts which avoid presupposing mind-body dualism. Gilbert Ryle criticizes the common view of the mind as a kind of "ghost in the machine"—an invisible, mythical entity, supposedly driving the body from somewhere within. John Searle focuses on mental states as simply a biological phenomenon connected with human brains. Reacting against the tendency of extreme materialists to ignore or explain away inner mental operations, Searle rejects being designated as a "materialist." However, he shares the basic characteristic of philosophical materialism: denying the existence of anything immaterial or spiritual.

While neurophysiologists can locate areas in the brain activated during mental activity, there are some areas of thinking for which special locations in the brain have *not* been found. No studies, for example, have determined where our *philosophical* knowledge is located. Even the philosophical knowledge of the materialistic monist, when he is theorizing about the non-existence of mind, is not traceable to any part of the brain or nervous system. Or, if a materialistic monist, in a weak moment, is thinking about his own thoughts, it is difficult to imagine the grey matter in the brain accomplishing this, bending back upon itself to catch itself in the act, producing materialistic self-consciousness.

Extreme idealist monists, who consider matter for all practical purposes non-existent, and reduce it to something mental or spiritual, are not as widely prevalent as materialists, since they strenuously oppose the acceptance of material realities that most of us take for granted. But they have existed in the history of philosophy and still exist. From the *idealistic* monistic point of view, everything is "virtual reality." The Dutch pantheist, Benedict (Baruch) Spinoza (1632–1677), argued that everything—including matter—is explainable as a mode or aspect of God, who is the one and only substantial reality. The Irish philosopher, Bishop George Berkeley (1685–1753), taught that physical existents which seem to exist in the external world are reducible to our perception of them (*esse est percipi*), caused by direct action of God on our mind. In Eastern philosophy, Hindus have often maintained that evil does not really exist in the world, but is *Maya,* an illusory appearance which can be overcome as one rises to higher spiritual states; and Mahayana Buddhism teaches that we can overcome subject-object dualism by attaining the insight that *consciousness only* exists.

(2) *Extreme dualism,* in contrast to all forms of extreme monism, asserts that a sharp dichotomy exists in humans between a spiritual or intellectual part, and a material or physical part. According to Plato—foreshadowing many contemporary "New Age" writers on "Near Death Experiences," and "reincarnation" theories—the human soul existed in a supernal world or "heaven" before it was implanted (or better, imprisoned) in a human body.

In early Christianity, St. Paul expressed the division between the "flesh" and the spirit in humans in *Romans* 7:15 by saying "the things that I would like to do, I do not do; and what I don't want to do, that I do." St. Augustine, elaborating on St. Paul's doctrine, explained that the reason for our failure to do the good things that we want to do is "original sin," inherited by all humans from Adam and Eve. The chief example of extreme dualism in modern philosophy comes to us from the French philosopher, René Descartes (1596–1650), who is famous for attempting to prove his own existence from the fact that he could think (*"cogito, ergo sum"*), and who then went on to argue for a sharp distinction between the mind or "thinking substance" (*res cogitans*) and corporeal things or "extended substance" (*res extensa*). He offers as an example the experience we have of waking up in the midst of a dream, where our consciousness of dreaming is obviously distinct from the dream-images in the brain (which are often immediately forgotten, out of the mind's grasp).

But Descartes's dualism led inevitably to the problem, how do body and mind come together and work together in a human being? Descartes conjectured, without any scientific evidence, that the pineal gland in the brain might be the point at which the interconnection of body and mind takes place. Contemporary dualists with a scientific bent are still looking for neural mechanisms in the brain that will answer Descartes's problem more definitively; but no breakthroughs have yet been reported.

6.3 Reflections on a Metaphysical Paradox

Unity—at least any *interesting* sort of unity—implies a duality or a multiplicity of some sort. We can speak of the "unity of X with X," but knowledge is not advanced, and the world yawns; but the "unity of X with Y" has the potential to be interesting. For example, the unity of oxygen with oxygen is taken for granted; but our study of the unity of oxygen with hydrogen or carbon is interesting, and advances our knowledge. Similarly, *duality*—at least any interesting duality—implies a unity. In other words, in order for there to be a difference between two things, they have to have something *in common*, so that they can be compared; and the more that they have in common, the more interesting is the difference. For example, there would be a difference between a window and the planet Mars, but this is not a very interesting difference; but the difference between identical twins or isotopes of the same element, is more interesting because less apparent, and advances our knowledge relatively to a greater degree. Finally, no such thing as *pure* unity or *pure* duality exists. Unity is always a unity of something with something else; and duality is always a duality of things with some common features. Thus when we discuss the human personality, it can be misleading and an oversimplification to describe it either in monistic or dualistic fashion. A description which explicitly characterizes the human psyche as a *unity-in-duality* would avoid extreme oversimplification and be more accurate.

6.4 Historical Philosophical Positions Emphasizing the Unity-in-Duality of Personality

(1) Aristotle—reacting against the Platonic notion (mentioned above) of the human soul as a separate "form" existing in another world and at some point imprisoned for a lifespan in a human body—emphasized the essential unity of the soul with the body. But the unity for Aristotle was a nuanced unity, a unity-in-duality. The nuance becomes clear in Aristotle's analogy of a statue: Just as a unity-in-distinction of form *and* content is discernible in a statue, so also the human soul is the "form" responsible for imposing distinctively human characteristics on the special physical organism, the human body, which serves as "content." Just like the case of the statue, in the human psyche one cannot pinpoint some specific point of separation between soul and body; but they are distinct as form and content.

Because of the unique interrelationship of a particular body with a particular soul, Aristotle opposed the Platonic theory of reincarnation—one can't just put any soul in any randomly chosen body, since body and soul are correlatives, essentially related to each other. Likewise, because of the interdependence of body and soul, Aristotle expressed doubt about the possibility of individual immortality with personal memories; the existence of the soul without a body (a"form" without a content) after death seemed to Aristotle metaphysically impossible, although "mind" as the supreme faculty of the soul would remain in an afterlife in some fashion—possibly as a non-individualized intellectual element.

(2) G.W.F. Hegel focused on the unity-in-duality of *spirit* as a synthetic notion, differing in its meaning from ideas like "soul" and "mind." Hegel discussed spirit both as an individual phenomenon, and in a more general sense, as something that pervades history and societies. In the individual sense, the human spirit as it evolves splits itself up into body and soul, and reunifies itself, creating personalities. This is a dynamic process that is constantly ongoing. Our individual experience involves a constant oscillation between the sense of distinctness of soul and body, subjectivity and objectivity, and the sense of unification of these opposites.

(3) Søren Kierkegaard rejected the Hegelian idea of spirit in a general sense pervading society, and reformulated Hegel's notion of the individual spirit. Kierkegaard speaks instead of the *self*, which is not a thing or substance but a *relation* between the two aspects which it synthesizes—the finite and the infinite. In other words, human beings are a paradoxical combination of the body, relating to the finite, and the soul, relating to the infinite; and human experience involves the continual distinction, balancing and coordination of these two distinct but complementary aspects of the self.

These three theories offer us examples of a middle ground between the extremes of monism and dualism. They lead us to the more complex, but not contradictory, conclusion that humans are *both* a unity *and* a duality.

6.5 Mind-Body Causality and the Problem of the "Prime Analogate"

Examples were given at the outset of this chapter of our common experiences of mind-body causality—either cases in which bodily states have certain effects on mental states, or cases in which states of mind or beliefs cause bodily changes. But an unavoidable problem needs to be addressed, connected with our use of "causal" language to describe these experiences: Causality in the strict sense is on a purely physical level—one physical object, for example, a billiard ball, bringing about a change of state in another; or some physical force, for example, heat or electricity, bringing about changes in bodies or spaces. But *if we distinguish the mental from the physical*, and refer to causal interactions *between* the mental and the physical, we are obviously not using the term, "causality," in the usual sense, but only in an analogous sense. In other words, we are talking about it as something analogous with physical causality. In this situation, physical causality is the "prime analogate," the primary way in which we use the term, "causality"; and other usages, for example, causal influences of the mind upon the body, or the causal influence that one idea can have on another idea, are "secondary" extensions of the primary meaning.

We move from primary to secondary analogates frequently. For example, "health" is primarily a state of a physical organism. But we can also speak in a secondary sense of vegetables or sunshine or a rosy complexion or political stability as being "healthy." And "black" is primarily a physical color, but we can also speak of "black humor," or financial accounts "being in the black instead of the red." Are we to conclude that mental-physical causality is somewhat similar to ordinary, real causality, but not really causality in the strict sense? Just analogous?

An alternative possibility would be to take *physical-mental* causality as the prime analogate! In other words, we might consider physical-mental causality to be the main form of causality in the world as a whole, the form of causality that people in general (including scientists and philosophers) are most familiar with, since in our daily lives we have hundreds of experiences in which the mind is having an effect on the body, or vice versa. As the physicist, Arthur Compton, remarked in his Terry Lectures at Yale, the evidence we have that we can move our little finger at will is immensely greater than all the evidence on behalf of Newton's laws. If we took this basic experience as our prime analogate, we would then have to speak in a secondary sense of things in the physical world bringing about changes in other physical things, or even of one idea (a mental "object") having an effect on other ideas.

In any case, we should be aware that *if strictly physical causality remains as our prime analogate*, the linguistic phenomenon of analogous references is responsible for the perplexing questions that occur if we presuppose that the mind is truly *distinct* from the body: If it is not bodily, how can it have a "causal" influence? *Where* is the mind (since a cause in the usual sense has to be located somewhere)? *At what time* does the influence take place? And, what is the *point of connection* between the mind and the body (Descartes's question, revisited), since causes ordinarily have to come into contact in some way at some place with the things they are having an effect on?

7

Human Freedom

Man has free choice. Or otherwise counsels, exhortations, commands, prohibitions, rewards and punishments would be in vain.

—THOMAS AQUINAS, *Summa Theologiae*

The history of the world is none other than the progress of the consciousness of freedom.

—G.W.F. HEGEL, *Philosophy of History*

Our first act of freedom, if we are free, ought in all inward propriety to be to affirm that we are free.

—Willliam James, "The Dilemma of Determinism," in *Pragmatism*

Man is condemned to be free. Condemned, because he did not create himself, yet is nevertheless at liberty, and from the moment he is thrown into this world he is responsible for everything he does.

—JEAN-PAUL SARTRE, *Existentialism.*

The main meaning of freedom, as defined by most dictionaries, is the "absence of restraint." And this definition appears to coincide with our shared experience. Our conviction of freedom becomes accentuated primarily under *negative* circumstances. A person who is imprisoned thinks of nothing but freedom, and we who are not subject to such confinement consider ourselves to have a quality not possessed by the prisoner. But imprisonment is just the most concrete and obvious example of constraints. Someone who is subjected to force or violence experiences unfreedom in the sense of a radical limitation of their power of movement and action. Persons afflicted with incurable handicaps sense a permanent limitation of freedom, while those with acute illness, such as flu with a high fever, experience a temporary limitation. A drug-induced lethargy, as well as certain paralyzing or immobilizing drugs used to treat some illnesses, have a similar effect. Possibly the most dramatic example of a clear negative notion of freedom is in cases of stroke, where a patient may be conscious but cannot activate his or her limbs or vocal cords. Such experiences seem inimical to freedom, since most of us presuppose that we should be able to initiate movement by mental commands; and this basically "dualistic" experience (our psyche divided on the one hand into a controlling, choosing, initiating part, and, on the other hand, into a controlled part) is a fundamental source for our notion of freedom.

7.1 Materialists and the Idea of Freedom

John Martin Fischer, in *The Metaphysics of Free Will*, proposes a thought-experiment. Suppose that a consortium of experts finally proved beyond the shadow of a doubt that everything in the world could be explained by previous events and the laws of nature. If we overcame our initial skepticism, would we still believe that we had free will, and had moral responsibility for our actions, and could make judgments about the responsibility of others? A conscious individual who is not impeded by any of the restraints mentioned in the last paragraph would probably hold on to this belief, since it is part and parcel of our concept of personhood.

Materialists often say they believe in the existence of free will, but there are difficulties in the way of reconciling materialism with free will. The materialist's claim seems to be based on proprioper-ception, the experience of what goes on in our own psyches—in particular, the almost universally shared experience we have of "being in control," initiating movements in ourselves and objects outside ourselves, making decisions, resisting unwanted feelings or distractions, and so forth. But these are psychological grounds, and the question about where such proprioperceptive experience comes from still remains. Consistent materialists, completely rul-ing out any non-material "self" as a mythical homunculus, will agree that their very existence is the result of environmental and hereditary factors, plus everything that has taken place in their past history, plus all the chance events of "natural selection," that led to the development of *Homo sapiens*, plus the infinite number of lucky events that apparently took place after the Big Bang to place humans in the right spot in the cosmos for carbon-based life to flourish. But how can anyone standing at the end of this incredible chain of physical causes and effects still maintain that they are not wholly determined by these things, that they still har-bor some elements in the psyche called "free will," which escapes all these determinations? Some point to quantum physics, which has proven that there are "indeterminacies" in the interaction of microparticles—effects that seem not to be subject to the usual physical laws—particles being transformed into waves and vice versa, photons which seem to decide at the last minute which slit they want to go into, and so forth. The idea is that there is a fun-damental indeterminacy at the atomic and subatomic level which, in the brain of even the most inveterate materialist, can help him or her to escape in some fashion from all the chains of determi-nations just mentioned—that is, to do or think things, or react, in ways not predictable from such determinations. But many quan-tum physicists point out that the indeterminacies of quantum mechanics are second-order phenomena, which appear on the screens of sophisticated apparatus. The operator of the apparatus is not actually observing first-order microphysical events, but wave-functions tabulated in terms of statistical probability. And even if the first-order particle interactions in the brain of a mate-rialist were completely indeterminate, any result on the brain would likely be chaotic or even bizarre operations, rather than "controlled activity."

7.2 Consequences of the Rejection of the Idea of Freedom

But it seems that, if someone is not free to decide whether they will commit a crime or not, they should not be held responsible for their acts. Materialists may have no problem with imprisoning criminals or even executing them, if they believe this will help protect the public at large; but, if they are at all consistent with their beliefs, they will refrain from saying or even judging that murder, arson, rape, or burglary are "wrong"—unless they want to "deconstruct" the term, "wrong," to mean "something disapproved by most people," or "something we will punish you for." For no act is criminal (or meritorious, or honorable) for a person, if they have no other choice. In fact, completely consistent materialist parents, for example, will never tell their children (and mean it) that what they are doing is wrong (unless "wrong" is simply redefined as "doing what I don't want you to do"), and will avoid praising or commending them, since the children have no other choice(s). On the other hand, if praise and blame have any meaning at all, and if we can speak sensibly about personal responsibility, freedom has to be presupposed.

7.3 Clarification of Terms

(1) *"Free choice"*. Unfortunately when we hear mention of "choice" or "the right to choose" in contemporary American culture we tend to think of a woman's legal choice of having an abortion or not, or (in some states) of the politically charged issue of government vouchers for tuition in public or non-public schools. But everyone knows that choice has much wider meanings than this—for example, the choice to have sex or not, to send children to school outside the home or not, the choice to vote Republican or Democrat, and the infinite other situations in which an individual in making a decision has more than one alternative.

(2) *"Free will"* implies something more than merely making a choice. The exercise of free will implies personal commitment and involvement in the choice being made, as well as a lack of exter-

nal or internal forces influencing one's decision. For example, a woman might make a choice of bringing a pregnancy to full term because of pressures from her husband or family to keep the baby; or to have an abortion because of pressures from a boyfriend to abort the baby. In either case, free will may be lacking because of external pressures. Likewise internal forces such as fear or love or passion can diminish the possibility of free-will choices. For example, a woman might go through with a pregnancy just because of her personal fear of abortion: the occasional risks with abortion procedures or fear of physical or psychological aftereffects; or a woman might choose to have an abortion not out of free will but just because of fear of public disapproval if she is unmarried, or just because of the possibility of losing her job because of the necessity of requesting a maternity leave. In sum, free will could be deficient or non-existent in any free choice that a person makes.

(3) *Liberty, or "political freedom"* goes beyond the parameters of individual free choice and free will, supplying the larger context which promotes and guarantees political choices and free-will involvement. For example, women in the Soviet Union, a totalitarian state, always had the freedom of having an abortion if they wanted it. This was a free choice, and probably even in many cases an expression of free will. But very few of us living in a democratic system would claim that the Soviets also had political freedom—which we would connect with constitutional guarantees of free speech and the right to join political parties, vote for candidates of the opposition, or even to choose to remain a citizen of the USSR, or to emigrate.

7.4 Conceptual Analysis

(1) *Free choice.* If we were to discuss the "existence" of rain tomorrow, someone with a logical bent would probably correct us and emphasize that rain tomorrow is not something existent but a possibility. So also, we are not concerned here specifically with the *existence* of free choice, but instead with its *possibility*. In fact, free choice is *by definition* a possibility instead of something actually

existing—the possibility of choosing X instead of Y (or Z, or any other alternative). For example, if choice X is for me to remain standing instead of sitting down (choice Y) at this moment, this is a free choice not because I actually chose X but because I *could have chosen* Y. The unavoidable problem connected with this experience is that we can only talk about the "possibility" of choosing Y after we have *de facto* already chosen X!

But how do we know that we could have chosen Y? There are two sources for this conviction: (a) *Logical possibility*: Anything is *logically* possible as long as it does not involve a logical contradiction. For example, no one has a choice of drawing a square circle, or walking without moving, or being in two places at the same time, because such choices are logically impossible. If choice Y is to sit down while still standing up, it would be logically impossible. But most choices fortunately are not like this; they are logically possible. (b) *Psychic withdrawal*: Just as we are constantly focusing our eyes on some things and "bracketing out" our vision of the other objects that may be nearby, so also we are able to withdraw our conscious attention from things or events in our environment. For example, a person in conversation with someone at a party, surrounded by loud music, laughter, and talking nearby, can psychically withdraw his or her attention from the surroundings, and may not remember anything except the conversation being engaged in; or a student physically present and awake in a classroom may "tune out" everything that the instructor is saying, due to boredom, daydreaming, or desire to study for another class. So also, when an individual is faced with X as one alternative, he or she is often not immersed in X, but can withdraw psychically from X at least enough to consider Y (or Z) as another alternative. The voter in a voting booth may be oscillating back and forth about whether to choose candidate X or candidate Y; but after voting for X is conscious that he or she could have voted for Y. Thus free choice in this sense is called *indetermination*, since he or she was not *determined* by X as something with a subjectively overwhelming influence, leaving no room for consideration of other alternatives. The feeling of indetermination with regard to alternatives does not, of course, prove that we actually chose an alternative, but only that we could have possibly done so. And our claim of having free choice is essentially the opening up of that possibility.

(2) *Free will.* As mentioned above, a free choice can be made even in a situation where a person encounters internal or external pressures, as long as he or she has the possibility of choosing otherwise, i.e. choosing Y instead of the X which is actually chosen. But for this choice to qualify as a free-will choice, something more is required—not just *in*determination, not just the possibility of choosing an alternative, but *self*-determination, a positive personal involvement emotionally or intellectually with the choice that is made. For example, the voter in the voting booth, not just oscillating between the choice of one candidate or the other, but enthusiastically voting for his or her favorite, may even feel disappointed at not being able to do more to advance the candidacy of their favorite. It is one thing to be *open* to, but *undetermined* by, X or Y; it is quite another thing to be *self*-determined to X or Y.

The concept of free choice is predominately *negative*. Even if there are strong conditioning pressures, I am not forced to choose X, I do have other options. But the concept of free will is *positive*— I have the feeling of positive involvement with X, based on full knowledge of X, not just "theoretical" knowledge but a knowledge that is practically-involved and even "biased" (in a good sense); an emotional component exists in such a situation, that translates into something like, "*yes*, this is me!" For example, a student may go to all of his or her classes out of free choice, but the involvement in these classes may differ widely—some may be experienced as boring, but attended because they are required; others may be anticipated enthusiastically, because of personal interests or pedagogical styles.

But how can we *know* that this is not just a matter of feeling, and that we really do have free will? According to William James, the source of our conviction that we act freely is from *effort-expenditure*, both physical and moral. *Physically*, why do athletes push themselves to the limits of their endurance, often with great pain? Just to get recognition? But very few get recognition. Quite likely, if we could put it into words, they want to gain the experience of being in control of their body, instead of the body being in control of them—of determining themselves, instead of being determined. *Moral* effort offers us even clearer evidence of free will. It involves going against external pressures, or one's own inclinations, to do the right thing—for example, being friendly to an acquaintance or blind date that you find obnoxious or unattractive. A prime example of moral effort is an act of self-sacrifice. Often completely unselfish acts are performed. For example, we can imagine someone without the possibility of public recognition giving up their life to save a stranger, possibly even an enemy. In such a case, they are not "determined" by the attractions of pleasure or friendship or the desire for fame. (Immanuel Kant objects that such apparently unselfish acts could be selfish for a religious person who hopes to gain a special reward in the afterlife for this act of bravery; so we might have to narrow down the example to the possibility of an atheist who enjoys life and has no desire to get relief from pain by dying!) But if we can conceive the possibility of such extreme examples of effort-expenditure, this thought-experiment offers us subjective or psychological evidence for our conviction that we are self-determined. If someone objects that even in such envisioned cases humans are still not self-determined, we can only ask for some clear explanation of *what* they are determined by in such cases, if not by the *self*?

(3) *Political freedom, or liberty,* is sometimes equated with "liberation" or "emancipation," but it is *not* the same thing; liberty requires much more than liberation or emancipation. If, for example, a nineteenth-century slave-owner decided to let his slaves go free, without property, perhaps without means to support their families, or separately from their family, in a state where they did not have the protections of citizenship, they would have many possibilities for free choice (where to go, where to look for a job, how to find shelter), but not political freedom. For political freedom requires a great deal of organization and structuring. It would be a mistake to construe political freedom as abstract possibility. In the nineteenth century, Horatio Alger's popular stories for boys promoted the idea that any young man can make whatever he wants of himself, with hard work and perseverance, in spite of all adverse circumstances. But this is an oversimplification that takes

no account of the number and degree of adverse circumstances or individual physical or mental handicaps. The ideal of "equality of opportunity" also sometimes falls into the category of mere abstract possibility. For example, educational opportunities can be meaningless for someone who has to work long hours to support himself or his family; economic equalization through welfare programs without corresponding access to quality education will not promote liberty; and "equality under the law" can be irrelevant to someone who does not have the resources to hire a competent lawyer.

Political freedom in the strict sense presupposes the existence of instrumentalities conducive both to the possibilities of free choice and to the exercise of free will. On the most fundamental level, the political enhancement of *free choice* involves the ability to choose citizenship or renunciation of citizenship. Further enhancement may require democratization in regimes which are dictatorial or which prohibit multiple political parties or which allow multiple parties but use unfair tactics to keep one party in power. In modern democratic-type administrations, free choice is promoted primarily by the ability to choose representatives in legislative bodies. In contemporary American politics, specific partisan examples of attempts to enhance free-choice possibilities might include the "school choice" programs, and Medicare revisions by Congress in 2003, which allow a choice of insurance plans for obtaining prescription drugs.

Political policies and structures conducive to the exercise of *free will* help to assure not only that choices can be made, but that they can be made with maximum *commitment* and *spontaneity*, optimally even enthusiasm. In the American system, instrumentalities promoting free-will include the well-known triad from civics textbooks—*referenda* involving consultation with voters about public policies, *initiatives* allowing citizens to propose policies, and *recall* giving citizens the power to remove officials for inefficiency, incompetence or misconduct before expiration of their term in office. Constitutional rights of free speech, freedom of the press, and freedom of assembly also help citizens to go beyond minimal requirements of free choice, and promote free-will political involvement.

The French political philosopher, Jean-Jacques Rousseau (1712–1778) proposed that, after a "social contract" had been formed to establish political structures, the resulting government would have the sovereign authority to "force people to be free." G.W.F. Hegel discerned totalitarian overtones in this approach, if self-determination by citizens is left out of the equation, but recognized the applicability of this concept to representative government. He reformulated the Rousseauan paradox, describing the creation of a free political society as "determining ourselves to be determined." In this formula, Hegel was suggesting that citizens can create around themselves solid constitutional structures, conformable to the natural divisions and characteristics of a society, that will preserve and increase the freedom of all, and, in a sense, make it difficult (and even inexcusable) for anyone *not* to be free. A constitution, as the law of the land, is conducive to political liberty just to the extent that it maximizes free choice and free will for all citizens.

8

Human Development

Mind . . . reveals its independence of its corporeity in the fact that it can develop itself [prematurely]. Children often have a mental development far in advance of their years. . . . In general, however, it must be admitted that intellect does not come before its time. It is almost solely in the case of artistic talents that their premature appearance is an indication of excellence. On the other hand, the premature development of intelligence generally which has been observed in some children has not, as a rule, been followed by great intellectual distinction in manhood.

—HEGEL, *The Philosophy of Spirit*

If only we could know what was going on in a baby's mind while observing him in action we could certainly understand everything there is to psychology.

—JEAN PIAGET, "The First Year of Life of the Child."

What we are about to examine is something quite *opposite* to human freedom. No freedom is involved in the earliest stages of development in infancy; and the degrees of consciousness associated with an infant's development are largely predictable, not subject to human self-determination. In other words, our concentration in what follows is on *necessity* rather than freedom. The developing infant has neither free choice nor any other kind of freedom. Infancy is a paradigmatic example of *un*freedom. With the passage of time, the child and adolescent does arrive at freedom; but paradoxically this is also a matter of necessity. Humans are "programmed" for freedom.

The normal stages in human development have been charted by developmental psychology, a relatively new discipline, pioneered in the twentieth century by Erik Erikson, Arnold Gesell, the French psychologist Jean Piaget, and others. Advances have been made in the scientific study of human emotional, cognitive and ethical development as well as motor development and sexual development. Developmental psychology, however, is not an exact science; it is concerned with *average stages of development* that can be predicted to take place in the development of most infants, children and adolescents. These averages may also change from generation to generation, and for diverse cultural groups.

What is of particular interest for philosophy are the conclusions of developmental psychology that are relevant to the stages of *consciousness*. In this chapter, we will concentrate just on the data relevant to this special area of development.

8.1 Problems Connected with this Analysis

To some, the investigation of *consciousness* would sound like an impossible task. A behavioral psychologist, for instance, might balk at this objective, claiming that consciousness, whatever it is, is not accessible to any kind of empirical investigation or measurement. But there are problems of consistency for this point of view. Even those who don't believe it is possible to know anything about consciousness do make judgments about the states of consciousness in others—about whether other persons are happy or sad, lying or telling the truth, relaxed or nervous, patient or in a hurry. If, say, a behaviorist makes such judgments, are the judgments just reducible to "X is acting in such a way that usually indicates happiness, or telling the truth," or the like? Or can we really know what is going on in the mind of X? Can we really be certain, for example, that Hitler hated Jews, or that Mother Teresa loved the poor and the sick in India? Or can we psychoanalyze them and say they are just reacting to early influences from their family, or obeying unconscious compulsions? Clearly, even in the case of Hitler or Mother Teresa, we cannot have absolute certitude; for example, some have claimed that Hitler thought he had a moral duty to prevent racial contamination, and critics of Mother Teresa have alleged that she was so ambitious for success in her mission that she accepted massive funding from dictators. But even with doubts like this, we can in most cases attain a high probability of making a correct judgment about the states of consciousness of persons we know, or know about. And our goal in the following analysis of the development of human consciousness will be to attain the highest possible probability of correctness.

8.2 Procedural Aspects

In making judgments about the states of consciousness of other persons, we are drawing analogies from our own experiences and from any external manifestations connected with these experiences. For example, if we see someone ranting and raving on the street corner, we would ordinarily identify this, in our experience, with anger. In other words, we think that if we were acting like that, it would be connected with feelings of anger. A high probability exists that the other person is angry, although we do not have absolute certainty—the person we are observing might be insane, or just a psychological researcher testing how bystanders on the street react to apparently angry strangers, or a fraternity pledge whose initiation instructions required him to perform bizarre antics. Or if we see someone crying, we usually can safely conclude that the person is sad, but we all know that occasionally people cry for joy; that manipulative teenagers may turn on tears to avoid being punished or losing privileges; and ethically challenged students will cry about their grades in front of their teachers to win sympathy and a reconsideration.

With regard to the consciousness of infants, we start off with an initial incommunicado problem. The word, "infant," comes from the Latin *infans*, which means literally "speechless"—an apt description, and a disadvantage for our purposes, since they can't tell us what they are thinking or how they are feeling, especially in the early months when rapid developmental changes are taking place. But there is also an advantage connected with their speechlessness: unlike adults, they can't deceive us, can't intentionally give false impressions, can't purposely hide their feelings. Capitalizing on this advantage, our procedure in analysis of the development of consciousness in infants will be to consider some well-known changes in behavior, common developments, well-documented by researchers, and make deductions from these externals regarding the presumably connected "inner" states; in examining the later stages of childhood and adolescence, more data is available, but the possibility of individual deception and/or social conditioning increases.

8.3 The Stages of Consciousness, Infancy to Adolescence

The neonate. William James described the world of the newborn child, or "neonate," as "one big blooming buzzing Confusion." Psychologists now generally agree with this assessment. Visually, the neonate could qualify for certification as "legally blind." He or she doesn't have the ability to focus as we do; everything, near and far, is extremely blurred. We can't take for granted that the neonate makes any of the distinctions that we take for granted—distinguishing the chair from the table, the table from the floor, the cat from the rug, and so forth.

Sensation. It is difficult to find analogies in our experience to understand just how basic *sensation* is for a neonate. It is probably something like the experience we have when we think we hear a sound, but are not sure if it's "just our imagination"; or feel a pain, but are not sure if it's from an external cause or merely a physio-logical disturbance. This state in the neonate is called "coenesthe-sis" or the "global mass" experience, in which the distinction that we take for granted between subject and object, between ourselves and the world "out there," is not made at all. Something that we might consider to be an external disturbance—for example, a noise in the room which doesn't affect us bodily—can be a quite per-sonal, *internal* disruption for the neonate; what we adults would refer to as an individual subjective sensation, for example, a wet diaper, can take on rather global proportions (a wet world) at the stage of coenesthesis.

Perception. The terms, "perception" and "sensation" are some-times used interchangeably. "I have a sensation of heat" can mean roughly the same thing as "I have a perception of heat." But per-ception in the stricter sense goes beyond sensation insofar as it involves focusing on a specific object as a cluster of sensations—for example, perceiving an apple as a clustering of specific sensations like color, shape, taste, etc., or identifying a person in terms of our sensations of their size, weight, color, gender and facial configura-tion. An unavoidable subjective element complicates perception—Eskimos perceive many more sense qualities in snow than South Sea Islanders or even Wisconsinites, and a wine expert like Robert Parker will perceive many more sense qualities in a glass of wine than you or I. Obviously, the power of perception in *infants* is dependent on the gradually developing physical ability to focus one's eyes on distinct objects with multiple sense qualities. The first major evidence that we have for the existence of the power of perception in infants comes at about the age of six months when we see them overcoming their instinctive tendency to hold on to objects such as rattles or toys. The fact that they will spontaneously begin to release objects from their grasp indicates that they have begun to escape from coenesthesis, that they are beginning to dis-tinguish themselves from things which are external to them. During the second year, we usually get clear evidence of advancing perceptual powers, as the "toddler" shows persistence in finding out the names of things. As incessant questions like "what's this?," what's that?" are multiplied, we know that their perceptual ability is maturing, that they are advancing in their ability to distinguish multiple objects with multiple properties.

Memory. While perception is concerned with present time, memory is concerned with the past—a perception of particular things or specific events *as* past. In the second month, an infant normally shows signs of anticipation, when it is about to be fed, or held, or changed; or fussiness about delays in the things it looks forward to. This behavior implies a memory of previous feedings, previous hugs, etc. It should be noted that there is a special relativity of time as applied to infants as compared with adults, since the human sense of time is relative to the speed or slowness of bodily processes. Since physiological processes usually proceed at a much more rapid pace in infants than in elderly persons, the world outside the infant will be perceived as moving relatively slow in comparison to the rapid developments taking place in the infant, while the world appears to move relatively fast in comparison to the processes slowing down in an elderly person.

Imagination. While memory has to do with the past and perception with the present, imagination allows us to refashion and combine images in ways that show an ability to escape our dependence on the actual past and present, and even to project the future. When the toddler begins to engage in make-believe ("let's pretend") activities, we get the first indication that imagination is being exercised, although it may have emerged earlier. As the child develops, all thoughts about the future, and plans for the future, imply an active use of imagination. The daydreaming and fantasizing that teenagers are prone to is often looked down upon by adults; but these activities have a constructive aspect insofar as they indicate heightened powers of imagination, although perhaps not properly channeled. Reading fiction tends to be a greater stimulant for imagination than fictional portrayals in television or movies, insofar as the reader of a novel or short story has to form his or her own images, sometimes in the thousands, in following the story, whereas the images are supplied ready-made for the viewer of a television- or film-dramatization.

Understanding. While perception is concerned with particular objects or particular events, understanding goes beyond the particulars to form general concepts or principles. For example, if we study the theory of evolution or the theory of relativity, and come to understand it, our understanding does not require the perception of anything in particular. When I talk about "survival of the fittest" or "natural selection," I do not need to have in mind vertebrates or primates or any particular animal; and my understanding of the relative warping of space-time does not necessarily have to be related to any particular planet, star, galaxy, or span of time.

A two- or three-year-old-child is too young to understand extremely general concepts like "being" or "existence," and possibly too young to understand a broad generalization like "animal" or "plant"; but ordinarily will be quite comfortable with generalizations like "toy," "cat," or "house." Pre-teens will not only be capable of forming major generalizations, but will give practical evidence of their abilities in making collections of butterflies, shells, coins, stamps, dolls, car parts, or baseball cards—in other words, categorizing. In high school and college they will often become proficient with the sort of activity we characterize as "abstract reasoning"—abstract concepts in areas like mathematics, physics, philosophy, or logic.

Volition. Sometimes volition, or the power of willing, is referred to as "practical reason" or "practical intellect"; but everyone knows that intellectual comprehension does not necessarily lead to decision, desire, or action. Thus volition is best considered as a separate faculty which goes beyond mere understanding. If we define free will as self-determination, the logical follow-up question is "determination to *what*?" (what sort of *goals* are being freely chosen?). Thus an important sign of arrival at volition is goal-orientation, the ability to set goals. Goal-orientation obviously evolves according to age, and our initial strong evidence for it appears in the so-called "age of obstinacy," at around two to five years of age, when the parents or caregivers and the child begin to have *conflicting goals.* The "negative" behavior of the child who refuses to heed mandates such as "eat your vegetables" or "pick up your toys" or "kiss your Aunt Martha goodnight" at least gives fairly certain proof that he or she is setting personal goals. Parents at this juncture have the choice of clamping down and insisting on their own goals, which may have the effect of creating conformists, or in some cases, rebels! or being "laid-back" or permissive, laying the groundwork for some possibly regrettable situations in adolescence. Parents who decide to negotiate regarding non-prioritized goals have the possibility of getting continual concrete philosophical evidence of the existence of volition as the child develops, and his/her goals become more complex and subjected to periodic reexamination.

Self-awareness. The importance of self-awareness as perhaps the main distinguishing characteristic of humans was discussed in Chapter 1. We see an initial external manifestation of self-awareness in the infant at about the age of nine months, when resentment is shown if objects are taken away—for example, if a toy or a figurine is removed from the playpen. This resentment indicates that the infant considers the object to be a possession; and since having a personal possession implies a consciousness of one's own ego, we can infer the existence of a basic consciousness of self—a state of consciousness capable of being intensified in later development and throughout life. In puberty, major developments take place, connected with the rapid growth of the body and the development of secondary sex characteristics. In a sense, it is impossible for the pubescent *not* to be aware of himself or herself. At times the result is "self-consciousness" in a negative sense—shyness or awkwardness, attempts to cover up embarrassment with silliness, or "showing off." The next stage, adolescence, is marked by a *deeper* awareness of self. An external indication of this positive inner development may be a newfound appreciation of solitude, so that it is not unpleasant but enjoyable to be alone—not just for sleep or listening to the radio, but for getting one's thoughts together. Keeping a diary and writing poetry are sometimes the offshoot of such experiences.

Social extensivity. A social orientation ordinarily begins in the early stages of infancy, and will be manifested by the attempts of the infant to attract company—for example, crying or making noises or banging things to get attention. But perhaps the main stage at which the "need for other people" becomes evident is during puberty, when great emphasis is often placed on physical similarities—wearing similar clothes, shoes and jackets, having similar hairstyles, using similar slang expressions or interjections. The movement toward school uniforms even in some public schools may be an attempt to moderate the competitiveness and occasional aggressive behavior caused by the desire to be in fashion with one's peer group. The ability to accept *differences* in one's social interactions is hard to come by, and in some cases may never be attained. Freud speaks about the possibility of "arrested development"; an individual could be "frozen," in a sense, in the stage of peer conformism which is natural in puberty. Adolescents often get beyond this phase, however, to appreciate differences, enjoying friendships with those who are extremely different in background, personality and/or intellectual interests.

Although, for purposes of clarity, we have considered other-awareness separately from *self*-awareness, it should be pointed out that these two aspects are paradoxically interrelated. That is, other-awareness is not opposed to self-awareness, but is complementary, and even inseparable. Since the others are other *selves*, compared and contrasted with one's self, it would be impossible to advance in other-awareness without knowing more about oneself, or to advance in self-awareness without attaining a greater insight about others.

The aesthetic sense. The term "aesthetic" is most often used with reference to the "fine arts"—music, painting, sculpture, dancing, or poetry. In a wider sense it is also applied to other sorts of sophisticated sensory enjoyment—such as the appreciation of nature, architecture, and photography. Aside from occasional musical or artistic prodigies, intense aesthetic consciousness connected with the fine arts does not appear to develop in childhood. Adolescence and early adulthood are the stages in which a deep and intense susceptibility to aesthetic experiences often begins. The "oceanic experience" that Freud describes as a feeling of unity with the universe, overcoming the boundaries of one's ego, is common in late adolescence, possibly associated with religious experience for some persons. But probably the most important and the most common aesthetic experience during this period is the experience of romantic love, which goes beyond infatuation and is perceived as a synthesis of physical and psychological and spiritual aspects. In Western culture this has become the ideal, in dating and courtship, of finding an "other" who is not only physically attractive, but complementary in personality and intellect, sharing the same values and interests. The fact that this ideal is often not perfectly attained is a continuing theme in innumerable novels, plays and songs.

Ethical sense. As mentioned in Chapter 4, some controversy exists at present as to whether there are distinguishable male and female patterns in the development of ethical consciousness. Leaving aside such controversies for the moment, we will focus on stages which appear to be common to both sexes. Our first evidence for the beginning of an ethical sense comes, paradoxically enough, during the "age of obstinacy," characterized by sudden outbreaks of "negative" behavior, sometimes interpreted too quickly as antisocial or potentially deviant. In reality, the frequency of the "no's" during this phase is a sign of the onset of an ethical sense, since being able to say "no" intelligently, with reasons related to goals we have set for ourselves, is essential for ethical decision-making (simple conformity to rules could take place without any ethical consciousness). In puberty, ethical consciousness often takes the form of simple maxims such as "do good to those who do good to you" or "do what is necessary to get along with others and avoid disapproval." Later adolescence is often characterized by the awareness of the great complexity of ethical decisions; simple rules give way to the examination of intentions, contexts, etc. in their complexity. This process does not necessarily lead to indecisiveness; the result is often the development of more nuanced maxims such as "understand your abilities and cultivate them" and "try to understand those who are different than you without compromising your integrity."

With the attainment of ethical consciousness, nature (or natural necessity) has in a sense led to the attainment of enhanced decision-making powers, and the exercise of personal freedom. Thus further development of the adult, will optimally show more individual direction and control, and less predictable or "programmed" stages of development.

9

Maturity

Human good turns out to be activity of soul in conformity with excellence, and if there exists more than one excellence, in conformity with the best and most complete. . . . But we must add "in a complete life." For one swallow does not make a summer, nor does one day; and so too one day, or a short time, does not make a man blessed and happy. . . . Yet evidently happiness needs the external goods as well. . . . For the man who is very ugly in appearance or ill-born or solitary and childless is hardly happy, and perhaps a man would be still less so if he had thoroughly bad children or friends or had lost good children or friends by death. . . . Why then should we not say that he is happy who is active in conformity with complete excellence and is sufficiently equipped with external goods, not for some chance period but throughout a complete life?

—ARISTOTLE, *Nicomachean Ethics*

Human life has been divided into three or four ages, but also into five, into seven, and even into ten. Shakespeare, in *As You Like It*, championed the division into seven.

> All the world's a stage
> And all the men and women merely players.
> They have their exits and their entrances
> And one man in his time plays many parts,
> His acts being seven ages.

But it is undeniable that only the divisions into three and four have had any permanence in man's interpretations. Both are enshrined in Greece and in the Orient, as in the primitive Germanic background. Aristotle is a partisan of the simplest type—youth, maturity (or *akmé*), and old age.

—JOSE ORTEGA Y GASSET, *Man and Crisis*

The identity crisis . . . occurs in that period of the life cycle when each youth must forge for himself some central perspective and direction, some working unity, out of the effective remnants of his childhood and the hopes of his anticipated adulthood.

—ERIK ERIKSON, *Young Man Luther*

The previous chapter was concerned primarily with human development into the late teens and early twenties. Until recent decades, most of the research by developmental psychologists has been concerned with these relatively early stages, infancy to young adulthood. But development does not stop at young adulthood, and the present chapter is concerned with the question, what are the final, most significant states of consciousness attainable by humans? We are not so much concerned at this point with extraordinary states that are claimed by some to be achievable through meditation or religious exercises. Our inquiry is about the states normally attainable, by most persons, on the average. This question—for the young person—is about the future. And some future things are predictable.

9.1 Psychological Maturity

Erik Erikson, who is chiefly noted for his studies of childhood and adolescent development, characterized the final transition of youth to adulthood as a searching for "identity," frequently amid some role confusion. Around the age of twenty, progress toward maturity, according to Erikson, proceeds normally through three types of oscillation: "intimacy" versus "isolation," as the young adult begins to forge new personal relationships; "generativity" versus "stagnation," as he or she works out constructive contributions to be made to society; and "integrity" versus "despair," around the age of sixty, when the individual often faces crises about life-goals.

In recent decades, some developmental psychologists, following the lead of Erikson, have conducted specialized studies of later adult development. Daniel Levinson's pioneering study of males, *The Seasons of a Man's Life*, came to the conclusion that there are four major stages in later male development: (1) *The Dream*, in which the young man develops an attractive and energizing ideal about what he wants to become, and what he wants to do with his life; (2) *The Mentor Relationship*, which involves a usually temporary relationship with a more experienced person who "shows him the ropes" and counsels him as he enters into a career or profession; (3) *The Occupation*, a final or semifinal choice of an area for specialization and future development; and (4) *The Love Relationship*, a relationship to a helpmate and "significant other" (not usually the same person as the "mentor"), often leading to marriage. (The last three stages do not necessarily take place in chronological order.)

Levinson claimed that these stages are also applicable to females. In response to doubts about this claim, he collaborated with his wife, Judy Levinson, to publish a book on mature female development. Their book, *The Seasons of a Woman's Life*, explores the female counterparts to the above four stages, and also analyzes the different attitudes characterizing homemakers and women who work or have careers. Predictably, the Levinsons' investigations found that the homemakers often had problems regarding feelings about self-development, while working women experienced stress with regard to the "glass ceiling" obstacles to professional acceptance and promotion.

Gail Sheehy, influenced by Levinson, followed the converse line of research, beginning with the study of mature female development, and then branching out to make applications to males. Sheehy's first book, *Passages*, focused just on females. Her more recent book, *New Passages* concentrates on both males and females, and charts development for later stages, including octogenarians. She divides the development into three stages: (1) *Provisional Adulthood* (ages eighteen to thirty) in which the young man or woman is searching for opportunities with great energy; (2) *First Adulthood*, involving initial turbulence, but leading eventually to flourishing; and (3) *Second Adulthood*—a "mid-life crisis," caused by awareness of one's limitations in attaining goals, but often followed by increased productivity and wisdom acquired by experience.

9.2 Existential Maturity

Even if a person passes through all the normal stages mentioned by developmental psychologists, the issue of happiness, or fulfillment, proposed by Aristotle (in an epigraph for this chapter) will inevitably arise. A fundamental *philosophical* analysis of the concept of maturity will lead us to the question, what does it mean to *exist* as a human being? What does it mean to activate the full potential of human existence? As indicated above, we are not talking about unusual states of consciousness that may be attained by geniuses, prodigies, or saints; but about ordinary, normal states attainable by most people. A biological analogy may help to show the importance of understanding the most mature states attainable: It would be difficult to judge the development of an acorn, a caterpillar, or a lion cub, if we knew nothing about the mature state of these organisms. Knowledge of the final state of any organism helps us put all the earlier stages of development into context. For example, if your cute little lion cub pet is getting just a little aggressive, you should be aware of where this will normally lead! So also with human beings, a clear idea of what is possible for a mature human being can give direction and incentives to an individual in early or intermediate stages of development.

"To exist" for a human being implies at least three basic relationships: (1) to physical goods; (2) to other people; and (3) to oneself. The connection of these three relationships with human existence is sometimes manifest in our language. For example, (1) if someone is lacking basic physical goods, we might comment meaningfully that "X is barely existing"; (2) negative responses to our affection by another person might lead to the comment, "as far as X is concerned, I don't exist"; (3) someone embarrassed about their behavior might make the strange and apparently contradictory remark, "that wasn't me," which at least offers evidence of an acute negative consciousness of the relationship to self. None of these three types of relationships is simple and direct and final; all of them involve oscillations that continue throughout one's life, somewhat analogous to the oscillations that take place in the "age of obstinacy" discussed in the previous chapter, in which the child and the parents encounter the problem of co-ordinating their attraction for disparate goals, and often begin to "negotiate." In what follows, we will consider the types of oscillation that take place in each of these relationships. Extreme cases will be discussed, to help clarify the various relationships, and show that maturity usually involves finding a middle-ground between the extremes.

9.3 The Relationship to Physical Goods

Physical goods begin with one's own body. The extreme of excessive concern for one's physical health is exemplified by the hypochondriac who is obsessed with the possibility of disease or dysfunction in his body, or the "fitness freak" passionately pursuing the goal of a perfect body; while the other extreme is risky and life-threatening unconcern about one's physical well-being. Similar extremes occur with regard to physical attractiveness, leading to cases like the foppish "airhead" who cares only about the way he looks, and the slouch who has no concern for his appearance. In regard to physical possessions, we are all familiar with the common extreme of the rich person who is so distracted by all he has that he never develops his personality, character, or creativity, and becomes a social drone; the other extreme is the unmotivated, indifferent person who makes no effort to acquire the goods and tools that are necessary for defining his personality, and constructing a "living space" in which he can best contribute to family or community, or develop personal interests and talents.

9.4 The Relationship to Others

With regard to our social relationships, "to exist" largely means "to receive recognition from others." We want to "have our own space," privacy, but would suffer if no one paid any attention to us at all. The issue here is *not* hate; at least if someone hates me, they are taking notice of me; I am important—a high-priority object—for them. If everyone hated me, I would still have strong negative evidence of my existence. But my existence would definitely be called in question if everyone was completely indifferent to me, took not the slightest notice of me. William James in his *Psychology* proposes a thought-experiment that helps to show why this is the case, and to bring out our ongoing need for recognition:

> No more fiendish punishment could be devised, were such a thing physically possible, than that one should be turned loose in society

and remain absolutely unnoticed by all the members thereof. If no one turned round when we entered, answered when we spoke, or minded what we did, but if every person we met "cut us dead," and acted as if we were non-existing things, a kind of rage and impotent despair would before long well up in us, from which the cruelest bodily tortures would be a relief; for these would make us feel that, however bad might be our plight, we had not sunk to such a depth as to be unworthy of attention at all.

A medical condition called marasma offers confirmation of James's thought-experiment. It is a condition that emerged in orphanages in the first half of the twentieth century: A newborn infant would be fed and taken care of, physically, but not played with or talked to; many would unexpectedly begin to waste away physically for no apparent reason. In one foundling home, thirty percent of the infants died and most of the others were retarded in their development. Investigators found that such deaths could be avoided if the infants were picked up and held for a few minutes each day by the caregivers. The fact that the infants had previously received no attention apparently was the cause not only of a metaphorical death of consciousness but actual physical death.

Granted that recognition is essential, an excessive need for it leads to psychological dysfunction. The movie, *Zelig*, gives us a humorous example of the way that the desire to be accepted can lead to a chameleon-like conformism. Other dysfunctional possibilities, depending on temperament and circumstances, include ostentatiousness and boastfulness; someone may commit acts of violence to gain recognition from criminal groups with which one identifies. In view of the possibility of these abnormalities, we become aware that we must develop an ability to reject the unreasonable demands of others, must be willing at times to do things that we consider worthwhile, even without recognition, or even in the face of criticism.

9.5 The Relationship to Oneself

We sometimes hear recommendations about self-acceptance, in the form, "feel good about yourselves," but we all know that this can be carried too far—leading to conceit, smugness, inability to accept criticism, and unwillingness to change. It is quite possible for many people to feel *too* good about themselves. On the other hand, self-rejection, sometimes expressed as "low self-esteem," can also be deleterious, leading to dissatisfaction with self, depression, and suicidal inclinations.

We can avoid the harmful extremes in relating to ourselves by adjusting what psychologists call the "level of aspiration." Someone with a low level of aspiration avoids bothersome challenges in personal development by devising personal goals that are too easy to attain—for example, the talented person who sets his sights low because he is unwilling to take the necessary steps to develop his talents, or the person who accepts the very low standards of behavior of his peers instead of developing his own standards. But levels of aspiration can also be set too high, as in the case of the perfectionist who can't live up to his own unrealistic ideals, or would-be authors or artists who never sit down to write or paint because they are afraid of imperfections, or destroy what they have done before they can be exposed to public view. The middle ground which is optimal for mature development is always to have goals just a bit higher than where you are now, but not so high as to be futile or frustrating or impossible to achieve.

9.6 Objective Maturity versus Relative Maturity

The general rule, or objective norm, following from the above observations, is that the mature person is one who avoids extremes in all three areas discussed. The ongoing *oscillation* that takes place in all three of these relationships is not a defect, not an imperfect stage that one finally "graduates from" in later life, but an essential characteristic of maturity even in the middle-aged and the elderly. One does not "arrive" at maturity as a final state, but as a healthy and not completely predictable oscillation.

But it is also obvious that individuals may face substantial obstacles in achieving this objective norm—obstacles such as physical or mental handicaps, a history of parental domination or abuse, extreme poverty, or lack of education. With reference to

Levinson's criteria, mentioned above, we know that not everyone has a "dream," or a choice of occupations, or a good mentor, or has luck in love. Thus we have to reconsider and qualify the norms we have just discussed to take into account *relative, subjective situations*. Considering the sort of obstacles just brought up, an individual may be relatively mature, although he or she may be objectively immature, by overcoming many obstacles that others don't have. For example, someone who is an occupational or social failure, or has low self-esteem or has an unhealthy attitude toward possessions, may be quite mature *relatively*, in view of where he or she started from.

In view of the fact that we usually don't know all the circumstances and obstacles encountered in individual situations, how are we to judge maturity? A standard criterion commonly utilized by psychologists, sociologists and others, is love. The ability to love in a responsible and committed way, and accept love, may be a good "rule of thumb" for assessing maturity, and even compensate for areas of apparent immaturity. But what is meant by love? The nature and dynamics of love is discussed in the next chapter.

10

The Nature of Love

Without friends no one would choose to live, though he had all other goods.

—ARISTOTLE, *Nicomachean Ethics*

[Anthropomorphous apes] might insist that they were ready to aid their fellow-apes of the same troop in many ways, to risk their lives for them, and to take charge of their orphans; but they would be forced to acknowledge that disinterested love for all living creatures, the most noble attribute of man, was quite beyond their comprehension.

—CHARLES DARWIN, *The Descent of Man*

True love is an emotion which discharges itself in an activity that overcomes self-centredness by expending the self on people and on purposes beyond the self. It is an outward-going spiritual movement from the self towards the universe and towards the ultimate spiritual reality behind the universe.

—ARNOLD TOYNBEE, *Surviving the Future*

10.1 Cosmic Love

We tend to think of love as something that takes place between persons; but it has been suggested by both ancients and moderns that love in a broader sense also exists. The ancient Greek philosopher Empedocles (490–430 B.C.) theorized that Love was a cosmic force which at various cycles brought about unification and harmony in the elements and among living beings, while at other times the opposing force, Strife, brought about separation and destruction. Some modern theories present similar cosmological interpretations. Freud had a great admiration for Empedocles's theory, but instead of presenting the "big picture" of love in the cosmos in a top-down mode from the outer edges of the universe, like Empedocles, he started from the bottom. He portrayed love as a material force, present in the attraction of the elements for one another, then rising up through cellular life into more complex forms—sexual attraction, the mutual affection of parents and children, friendships, and various movements to unite communities and nations. In a similar vein, Teilhard de Chardin spoke of a "love energy" present in the atoms and molecules and evolving into the various forms of human love, and beyond this to an ultimate unification of mankind in a higher state of consciousness (discussed in Chapter 5). Such theories seem to suggest that love is a natural force that may, sooner or later, predominate in the world! But most philosophers and psychologists do not agree with, or focus on, such cosmic views of love. And for most of us, the most important thing is to understand love as a human phenomenon, as far as that is possible.

10.2 Interpersonal Love: Cultural Influences

Some contemporary cultural influences should first of all be recognized:

(1) *The equation of "love" with sexual relations.* In English, as well as other languages, a *prima facie* identification of love with sex is noticeable. "Making love" ordinarily means having sexual intercourse (although it is well-known that this can take place with little or no affection or love); a "love child" is a euphemism for the result of an unplanned pregnancy; a "love triangle" connotes jeal-

ousy and rivalry of two people for the sexual favors of another; and one's "lover" may be a "one night stand" whose name has been forgotten. We may conclude that there is no necessary relationship between sexual relations and love.

(2) *Emphasis on single bliss.* Novels, films, and poems are not much help in getting beyond a superficial and merely sexual interpretation of love. As represented in these media, love stories are typically pre-marital, extra-marital or post-marital, with occasional exceptions celebrating married love. The "Playboy Philosophy" carries this trend to an extreme, suggesting that if you want to maintain the excitement and thrill of love, you have to avoid marriage. This "philosophy" is a latecomer: Sartre and other existentialist philosophers were insisting on the disjunction of love from marriage early in the twentieth century. The steep divorce rate in the United States and many other Western countries appears to indicate that many people are finding that marriage is no love-paradise—divorce usually being a sign that one or both parties considered their union loveless. We might conclude from the statistics that our courtship and marriage customs are not very effective—possibly no more effective than the "arranged marriages" of yesteryear that still prevail in many parts of the world. On the other hand, the short-term "relationships" dotting the "singles" scene seem even less successful in promoting the cause of true love.

(3) *Heterosexual emphasis.* In many parts of the Western world it is difficult to talk about "love" between males. Many males, for fear of being branded homosexual, would feel embarrassed telling their best friend that they loved him. In Anglo-American culture affectionate physical contact—hugs and "European" kisses—among males has been traditionally relegated to some ethnic groups—Italians, Greeks, Hispanics, Middle-Easterners, some Slavs—or to some special occasions, for example, after winning a football game, or a reunion of father and son, or brothers, after an extended absence. So one might surmise that love is not only primarily for sexually attracted single people, but also primarily for people of the opposite sex. But we sense that there is something wrong with this assumption, and our unease may motivate us to re-examine our concept of love.

10.3 Philosophers and Love

Love has not been a favorite topic for investigation by philosophers. Investigation of knowledge has always been the priority. If we consult the latest online version of the *Philosopher's Index*, which indexes the philosophical books published and articles in philosophical journals since the 1940s, we find, for example that there are 26,874 entries in the subject-index regarding *knowledge*, as compared with 3,769 entries regarding *love*—over seven times as many entries. Does this have anything to do with the fact that most philosophers in the Western tradition have been men? Probably not, since even in recent decades when many women have joined the ranks of professional philosophers, the relative proportion of works on love has not changed significantly. Possibly philosophers are afraid to barge in on what has been considered poets' territory—the mysterious and the intensely passionate experiences of love which seem to transcend rational analyses. In any case, while many philosophers have specialized in the theory of knowledge (epistemology), no major philosopher has *specialized* in research on love. But fortunately a considerable number of psychologists have focused their attention primarily on this issue. We will make use of some of their ideas in the conceptual analysis that follows.

10.4 Love and Its Opposites (What Love Is *Not*)

(1) *Love versus knowledge.* According to Thomas Aquinas, the movement that takes place in love is just the opposite of the movements of knowledge. In knowledge, we in a sense change objects into ourselves, analogous to the way that we change food into our body by eating and digesting. To use a metaphor from physics, this is a "centripetal" process, in which objects and events outside of us are drawn into our consciousness and become subject to the categories and the interconnections controlled by consciousness. Love, on the other hand, is "centrifugal": we move outside ourselves to that which attracts us, and the process of love changes us into the object of our love. Thus, concludes Aquinas, it is better to love

God than to know him; for example, a simple and uneducated person with minimal knowledge but an intense love of God could easily be more perfect in love than a brilliant theologian or philosopher who knew everything there was to know about God. Also, conversely, it is better to know evil than to love it; for example, a member of the police vice-squad who works full-time with prostitutes and pimps, child pornographers, or drug lords, or someone who studies the motivations of hit-men or the various forms of child abuse or domestic violence, will not necessarily be sullied or compromised by any of these duties, unlike the person who loves or enjoys being involved in these sorts of things.

(2) *Love versus isolation.* According to Erich Fromm, love is the only thing that can help us to overcome the feeling of isolation; it is the only "natural" remedy for human isolation. "Artificial" counterfeits for love are frequently chosen—such as sex, drugs, or alcohol—since they help us, like love, to feel a temporary escape from ourselves; but the sense of isolation always returns in the aftermath. The expansion of the ego and the connection with others that takes place in love is lacking in those counterfeits. Fromm also emphasizes that love as an enhancement of the personality is *active*, not passive; although most of us want to *be* loved, it is in developing the ability to love others that we become habitually able to overcome our personal isolation.

(3) *Love versus existential anxiety.* Oswald Schwartz distinguishes existential anxiety from fear. Fear in the strict sense has a specific object, while existential anxiety (*Angst*) is just a deep and generalized psychological trembling that has no specific object. Comparisons are made to children's fear of the dark. The lack of a definite fearful object accentuates the feeling of distress. Love brings about a redirection, which counteracts the distress of anxiety, and provides the most positive and enduring release.

(4) *Love versus hate.* Freud distinguishes the life-instinct (*Eros*, libido, sexuality in a very wide sense) from the death-instinct (*Thanatos*, generalized aggression or destructiveness). But Freud as a psychoanalyst is also interested in the strange admixtures and complicated interactions of love and hate—for example, constantly harassing or demeaning someone whom you admire or are

attracted to, or who reflects a trait or desire that you have failed to cultivate, or repressed to your unconscious.

(5) *Love versus indifference.* Ignace Lepp disagrees with the common opinion, and also Freud's opinion, that the opposite of love is hate. According to Lepp, the most aggressive, demeaning assault on a person would be—not to show hate for them—but to completely ignore them. With hate, you are at least recognizing the existence of a person, and attaching some significance or negative importance to that person. Hate, as Freud argued, often disguises a hidden admiration or attraction; indifference involves no such admixture, and is characterized by a complete lack of love.

These theories are not mutually contradictory. It is possible, and even quite probable, that *all five* of the "opposites" just considered are outside the boundaries of love, and completely incompatible with love. Centered within these outer limits, and not to be confused with any of its opposites, love can be represented topographically as follows:

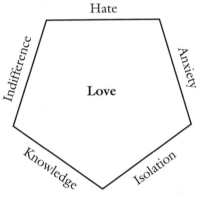

FIGURE 10.1   **Topography of Love**

10.5 What Love *Is*

The most obvious general identifying characteristic of love appears to be unity. If a cosmic love exists, as Empedocles thought, it would be a unifying force; love in the social sense has to do with the unification of individuals and the ability to stay in connection with others; love as an intrinsic psychological quality of an individual has to do with the avoidance of personal disintegration or the descent into one's own darkness. More specifically, love is . . .

Some kind of unity, but not the sort of unity associated with knowledge. Knowledge, like love, is a type of unity. When we know something, we have to come into contact with some object, by focusing on it or turning our attention to it, for knowledge to take place. But the main characteristic of knowledge is the presentation of something as "objective," represented as it is "in itself"—as distinct from ourselves and distinct from our subjective feelings or impressions about it. Love, in contrast, although *beginning* with a distinction from the loved object, ends with a joining or intermingling or fusion or identification with that object. The salient characteristic of love is the unification that it brings about. In other words, while knowledge is a unity-in-*distinction*, love is a *unity*-in-distinction.

Not the same as desire. "Love at first sight" is not love, although it may lead to real love. For love at first sight, as applied to a person, is not love for that person, but love for the *sight* of that person, his or her physical beauty, the initial impressions she or he makes in speaking, behavior, and suchlike. In other words, "love at first sight" for a person is an impossibility and a misnomer. It generates desire, and is synonymous with a type of desire; but love requires something more than this. Love involves a pursuit of the object of desire that leads to enjoyment of, or satisfaction in, that object. A "love" that is not primarily interested in enjoying or attaining its object in any way would more precisely be characterized as desire. For example, the desire for knowledge by no means indicates a love for knowledge; one who desires knowledge may never pursue it, or may try to get it without effort—for example, by listening to tapes while sleeping, or by direct infusion by God or angels—or may acquire just enough to satisfy some real love (such as for power or recognition).

10.6 The Types of Love

Aristotle in the discussion of friendship in his *Nicomachean Ethics*, Book 8, Chapter 2, distinguishes three types of love—love based on goodness, or utility, or pleasure:

Not everything seems to be loved but only the lovable, and this is good, pleasant, or useful. . . . Those who love for the sake of *utility* love for the sake of what is good for themselves, and those who love for the sake of *pleasure* do so for the sake of what is pleasant to themselves. . . . Perfect friendship is the friendship of men who are *good*, and alike in virtue.

The love of pleasure can exist on either an impersonal or a personal level. On the impersonal level, it has to do with the simple satisfaction of the senses of taste, smell, touch, sight and hearing, for instance, in eating or listening to music or watching a sunset; as well as activities which bring pleasure, for example, athletic competitions. The love for animals or pets that we enjoy brings us closer to the personal level. On the strictly personal level, persons can be loved just because they bring us pleasure—for example, because we enjoy conversing with them, or listening to their jokes, or having them as tennis partners or sexual partners.

The love of utility can also exist on an impersonal level. For example, I love my multipurpose Swiss pocket knife, and am never without it; I love my new computer, which allows me to surf through graphical web sites faster than anyone in my neighborhood; I love my faithful watchdog, or the drug-sniffing dog that I use in my police work, or the cows that produce income for my dairy farm. I can also love other persons as useful—such as the handyman who is always available to fix things in my house at a reasonable price, the mentor at work who is "showing me the ropes," the CPA who helps me make out my income tax return without getting audited.

The love of goodness, on the other hand, is always personal. Scenes in nature can have beauty, but not goodness; when we refer to music, paintings, objects of art, etc. as being "good," we are referring to the pleasure or utility they bring us, but they don't have goodness in the strict sense. But we *can* speak of the goodness, a.k.a. the virtue, of *persons*—an intrinsic quality which we ascribe to them, even if they do not bring us pleasure or are not useful to us in any way. This quality, as Aristotle observes, is hard to find; but it is the only viable basis for a close friendship, or for married love or close kinship relations which transcend motivations of pleasure or utility.

Romantic love. Much has been written about the genealogy of romantic love, its origin in the institution of medieval "courtly love," the effect of the eighteenth-century romantic movement, and the evolution of the love-ideal in novels and films. As it is conceptualized at present in Western culture, romantic love presents us with an ideal synthesis of all three of the above aspects—pleasure, usefulness, and goodness: The *romantic ideal* is a person who is physically attractive and sexually compatible, *and* able to assist us in our life's pursuits and work, *and* be a true friend, sharing the same values. This ideal, carried over into mate-selection and marriage, is obviously difficult to realize in an uncompromising way, and can place on marriage a load that does not exist in cultures not attuned to the Western romantic ideal.

Further extensions of the Aristotelian categories. Insofar as the *ecology* movement is associated with the love of nature, it exemplifies the love of pleasure (nature as an aesthetic object) and love based on utility (for example, keeping pollution out of the water we drink and the air we breathe). If one accepts a strong version of the "Gaia hypothesis" (which theorizes that the earth functions like a living organism), the ecology movement may possibly also imply a personality-oriented love of goodness. The love of *God* may also include any or all of these three types: God may be loved because of the pleasure one gets in prayer or acts of devotion or worship; or because of utility, if we feel that our prayers are answered, and our needs are addressed; or because of goodness, if the Divinity is simply perceived as a person and as infinitely good.

11

Philosophy and the Paranormal

Out of my experience, such as it is (and it is limited enough), one fixed conclusion dogmatically emerges, and that is this, that we with our lives are like islands in the sea, or like trees in the forest. The maple and the pine may whisper to each other with their leaves, and Conanicut and Newport hear each other's foghorns. But the trees also commingle their roots in the darkness underground, and the islands also hang together through the ocean's bottom. Just so there is a continuum of cosmic consciousness, against which our individuality builds but accidental fences, and into which our several minds plunge as into a mother-sea or reservoir. Our "normal" consciousness is circumscribed for adaptation to our external earthly environment, but the fence is weak in spots, and fitful influences from beyond leak in, showing the otherwise unverifiable common connection. . . . When was not the science of the future stirred to its conquering activities by the little rebellious exceptions to the science of the present? Hardly, as yet, has the surface of the facts called "psychic" begun to be scratched for scientific purposes. It is through following these facts, I am persuaded, that the greatest scientific conquests of the coming generation will be achieved. *Kühn ist das Mühen, herrlich der Lohn!* [Valiant the effort, magnificent the rewards.]

—WILLIAM JAMES, "The Final Impressions of a Psychical
    Researcher," *The American Magazine* (October 1909)

Love may be the highest attainment of human consciousness, as well as the best index of maturity. But presumably the ability to love is something attainable by most of us, a "normal" human power. Paranormal powers, or *Psi*, on the other hand, appear to be just beyond the limits of what most people can attain. But possibly they do exist, and are attainable for at least some gifted persons. To explore this possibility, in the late nineteenth century, the Society for Psychical Research (SPR) in Britain and the American Society for Psychical Research (ASPR) in the United States were founded by scientists and philosophers for the study of paranormal phenomena. The SPR, with international membership, currently publishes the *Journal* of the SPR, and their *Newsletter*, the ASPR publishes the *ASPR Journal*, their *Newsletter*, and the *Newsletter Supplement*. Since the founding of these societies, laboratory research on the paranormal has expanded considerably in the United States and many other countries.

11.1 Empirical Research on Paranormal Phenomena

The scientific study of parapsychological phenomena has been conducted over the years by many universities and research institutes. Some of the best-known include the Institute for Parapsychology, Rhine Research Center, at Duke University, Durham, North Carolina (www.rhine.org); Princeton Engineering Anomalies Research (PEAR) Laboratory at Princeton University (www .princeton.edu/~pear/), in operation from 1979 to 2007; the Division of Psychiatry at the University of Virginia (http: //www.healthsystem.virginia.edu/internet/personalitystudies/); the Consciousness Research Laboratory, Petaluma, California (www.parapsych.org); the Cognitive Sciences Laboratory, Palo Alto (www.lfr.org); the parapsychology section of the Psychology Department of the University of Hertfordshire, England (http://www.psy.herts.ac.uk); and the Koestler Parapsychology Unit, University of Edinburgh, Scotland (http://moebius.psy .ed.ac.uk/index.php3). A comprehensive list of laboratories worldwide can be found on the website of the SPR, http://www

.spr.ac.uk/resdir_World.html. In what follows, we will examine the current status of parapsychological research, the results (if any) of the research, and the philosophical implications.

11.2 Research Methodologies

One of the most important methodological concepts relevant to controlled experiments in the research centers is a principle of statistical probability, Mean Chance Expectation (MCE). A simple example of MCE would be the flipping of a coin—if a person flips a coin ten times, "heads" will come up about fifty percent of the time, if he flips it one hundred times, the result will be closer to fifty percent, and if he flips it a thousand times, the result will be even closer to fifty percent; and if a thousand people were to flip a coin simultaneously, "heads" would come up in a population quite close to fifty percent of the flippers. An unexplainable "anomaly" would exist if an individual were to flip a coin many times and "heads" would come up seventy percent of the time, or if a large number of people were to do this and "heads" would come up for seventy percent of them.

FIGURE 11.1 Zenner Symbols

Early experiments in the Rhine Research Center and elsewhere made use of MCE in developing the "Zenner Cards" with five cards each of five different symbols, so that the MCE in guessing the right card, purely by chance, would be close to 5.0, since there is a one-fifth probability that each of the twenty-five cards will be guessed correctly. More sophisticated uses of MCE were later devised, as we shall see.

11.3 Major Types of Psi

Precognition is perception of future events as if they were present. If a prediction is made on the basis of such supposed perceptions, these can be short-term predictions—for example, of an event that will take place tomorrow; or (alleged) long-term predictions—for example, the predictions of the coming of a Messiah by Old Testament prophets such as Isaiah and Jeremiah, or the predictions of twentieth-century events by the medieval seer Nostradamus, or the predictions of all the popes to the end of the world (there is only one left after Benedict XVI!) by St. Malachy O'Morgain in the twelfth century. Precognition is difficult to test when it is phrased in vague symbols or metaphors (as is the case with the predictions of Nostradamus and St. Malachy), but relatively easy to test scientifically if specific factual events are predicted. A prediction is made, and if it comes true, a "hit" is recorded. In the laboratory, Zenner cards were initially used to test precognition. The subject being tested was typically asked to predict what the order of the cards would be after they were shuffled. More recently, computers that can put series in random order have been used; subjects are asked to predict how a series will be ordered after it has been randomly reordered.

Retrocognition, as the name indicates, is the opposite of precognition—a perception of past events as if they were present. In one famous case, two British teachers, Eleanor Jourdain and Annie Moberly, on vacation in France, visited the gardens at Versailles in 1901 and claimed to witness events that took place during the 1770s just prior to the French Revolution. Their book, *The Adventure*, dramatized for TV by PBS in 1983, is a detailed account of what they saw. Retrocognitive psychics have sometimes been commissioned by police departments to help reconstruct crime scenes.

Clairvoyance (from the French, "to see clearly") is the perception of things or events that are not present in the normal way to the five senses, especially the sense of sight. Some of the accounts of supernatural happenings in the New Testament may also be categorized as descriptions of clairvoyance—for example, the account in *Matthew* 17:27, when Peter asked how to pay the tax collector, and was told by Jesus to catch a fish and check for the coin that would be in the fish's mouth; or the account in *Luke* 19:26 about Jesus's knowing that there would be a donkey waiting for him in a neighboring town; or Jesus's clairvoyant perception of Nathaniel under a fig tree in *John* 1:50. The most famous clairvoyant in history is the Swedish spiritualist Emanuel Swedenborg (1688–1672), whose visions even included the spirit world—leading Kant to write a book, *Dreams of a Spirit Seer* to debunk Swedenborg's metaphysical claims. The most common claims of clairvoyance have to do with "Spontaneous Psi Phenomena." The APRS (mentioned above) was initially founded to investigate such claims. Such phenomena include sudden intimations by visions, dreams, or auditory messages, of the death or grave danger of a relative or friend, or of future events; or unexpected material events, such as the stopping of a clock at the time of someone's death; or seeing "poltergeists." Parapsychologists such as Louisa Rhine have conducted surveys of reports of such phenomena, and polling organizations have surveyed frequencies of these experiences in many countries.

Clairvoyants are sometimes employed in detective work, to locate the bodies of crime victims. Zenner cards have been used to test for clairvoyance, by asking subjects to identify cards placed face down or in another room. More recent laboratory investigations of clairvoyance utilize *Remote Viewing* methodology. "Remote viewing" is a term coined by Russell Targ and Harold Puthoff to describe the sort of experiments they conducted at the Stanford Research Institute during the 1970s. These experiments sometimes involved placing a randomly chosen photo in a remote location and asking a psychic subject to describe it; at other times a psychic subject would be asked to describe a remote location after being given the geographic co-ordinates. Similar experiments on "precognitive remote perception" have also been performed by the Princeton Engineering Anomalies Research group.

Clairaudience, as the name indicates, is the audial counterpart of clairvoyance.

Telepathy (from the Greek, "reception at a distance") is the ability to read thoughts of another person. According to Gallup polls in 2001 and 2005, over thirty percent of Americans believe in telepathy; and, according to the Gallup and Newport poll of 1991, twenty-five percent of Americans claim to have had telepathic experiences. The New Testament seems to report a telepathic experience in *John* 8:7, when Scribes and Pharisees wanted to stone an adulteress, Jesus began writing on the ground (usually interpreted as listing the sins of the accusers) and caused the accusers to walk away; and in *Acts* 5:1–10, in which the Apostle Peter seems to read the minds of Ananias and Sapphira, who were lying about their possessions.

Both the United States and the Soviet Union during the Cold War were interested in the possibility of using telepathy for military purposes—for example, for guiding missiles. Captain Edgar Mitchell carried out an experiment during the Apollo 14 flight to the moon in 1971, trying to transmit two hundred number sequences to four recipients on earth. A couple of the transmissions were statistically interesting, but the experiment as a whole was not spectacularly successful in proving the possibility of telepathy.

Testing with Zenner cards has been inconclusive, since what appears to be a telepathic transmission of a Zenner symbol could be in reality a case of clairvoyance of a card or precognition of what card would be transmitted. To facilitate properly controlled thought-transmission special environments called "Ganzfelds" have been constructed (*Ganzfeld* in German means a "whole or undivided field"). In the Ganzfeld, usually two separate soundproof rooms are provided for the sender and the receiver, in such a way that distractions are kept to a minimum; the eyes of the receiver are covered, and the sender periodically tries to transmit images seen on a screen. Afterwards the receiver is taken out of the Ganzfeld and shown four images or videos, and has to choose the one that was sent telepathically. The MCE for "hits" in this experiment is twenty-five percent, but the average of seven hundred sessions conducted by twenty-four investigators produced a statistically significant average of thirty-four percent.

ESP is a general term which designates any of the preceding types of cognition. Some researchers object that the term is inappropriate, since "Extra-Sensory Perception" seems to imply that some types of perception might actually exist outside the normal parameters of the five senses. Thus some laboratories choose to describe their research as a study of "anomalous cognition"—that is, types of cognition for which we have no reliable explanation at present.

GESP is a general term for ambiguous results; it is used to indicate that some cognitive phenomena cannot be precisely defined as telepathy, clairvoyance, or something else. For example, if tests for telepathy are conducted with positive results in a Ganzfeld, as described above, the researchers may not be certain that the results are evidence of telepathy instead of clairvoyance (unintended perception by the receiver of the images on the screen in the other room, instead of the intended reception of the thoughts transmitted by the sender).

Psychokinesis (PK) literally means "movement by the mind." While ESP is concerned with paranormal perception of objects or events, PK designates an ability to exert some kind of purely mental control over the physical state of objects or events. Stage demonstrations by alleged psychokinetics (for example, Uri Geller) often involve bending spoons or nails, making objects move, or raising the temperature of heat-recording instruments one or two degrees. Early studies of PK by parapsychologists involved tests of subjects trying to influence the throw of dice or causing coins to flip heads or tails more often than the MCE. More recent testing utilizes Random Number Generators (RNGs), which listen for electronic or radioactive "noise," then convert this by computer into random numbers; the subject of the test tries to mentally change the distribution of numbers so that it is no longer random. A 1989 database of these experiments showed that sixty researchers reported results with an average statistical deviation of fifteen standard errors from chance.

"*Bio-PK*" implies the ability to exercise mental effects on external living organisms. This has been tested by researchers using a method called Direct Mental Interactions with Living

Systems (DMILS). In these tests, typically a "starer" and a "staree" are isolated but monitored by a closed-circuit video connection. The staree's nervous system is monitored to see what effects staring has on him or her. Some evidence exists that being stared at can significantly activate or calm that person's nervous system (the starer is given instructions as to what effect he or she should try to cause).

Mediumship is the alleged communication with deceased persons by "mediums," who either make the contact directly or indirectly through "controls" or spirit guides, in "seances" held for living persons interested in making contact with "the other side." "Physical" mediums are noted for producing "materializations" of persons or objects. Almost all scientific investigations of physical mediumship have produced evidence of fraud. "Trance" mediums claim to receive and transmit messages from deceased persons to the "sitters" participating in the seance. Some of the successes of trance mediums—for example, transmitting information that supposedly only a deceased person or the person being addressed would know—might be reducible to clairvoyance or telepathic powers possessed by the medium.

11.4 Philosophical Issues Connected with Psi

"Supernatural" versus preternatural and paranormal. Some examples were given above of apparently paranormal events narrated in the Bible; but the choice of these examples was necessarily quite selective. Other major events reported in the Bible—Moses drying up a path through the Red Sea so that the Hebrews could pass through, Old Testament prophets predicting the circumstances for the coming of a Messiah several centuries later, Jesus raising Lazarus from the dead after the body had already started to corrupt—go beyond what we call the "paranormal"—that is, the "normal" paranormal. Such miracles, if they really took place, and such prophecies, if they were really made and fulfilled, go beyond what is usually meant in current research by clairvoyance, precognition, or PK. In such cases, there would be a significant difference of degree, which would still remain

unexplainable, even if parapsychological laboratories were successful in verifying some of the more "normal" forms of Psi discussed above.

The question of existence. Sometimes scientific investigations are concerned with whether or not some specific thing or phenomenon *exists*. For example, physicists for many years were searching for (and finally found) a cosmic radiation belt, which would give evidence for an original "big bang" whose explosion or expansion created the galaxies of the universe; and quantum physicists now are searching for the existence of a hypothesized "Higgs boson," which if found would presumably help to explain some mysteries in the microcosm, such as particle mass or lack of mass. But in investigating Psi we are looking not for the existence of some thing or event, but for the existence of a specific power in individuals. An analogous case would be if some investigators doubted the ability of Karate masters to chop bricks in half with their bare hands, and then conducted tests to verify this power; or if investigators doubted that yogic gurus in advanced states of meditation could actually defeat gravity by levitation, as they claim. Methodologies for the investigation of single acts of this sort could be developed without too great difficulty. Methodology for the investigation of innate capacities of some gifted subject for ESP or PK turns out to be more complex. Just one case where a subject successfully describes what is in a distant room, or guesses what a laboratory tester is thinking, or causes dice to be cast with a certain number, or even causes the temperature on a gauge to rise one degree, would not give evidence of unusual psychic powers; such a case could be attributed to coincidence or to fraud. Thus many instances would have to be examined, and the successes would have to be repeated over and over again in such a way as to go beyond statistical probability, or the MCE.

Some parapsychologists have maintained that through controlled experiments they have identified subjects who can consistently defeat the MCE. But how can we eliminate the possibility of fraud, either on the part of the investigators or on the part of the subjects? Critics of parapsychology, including most "mainstream" psychologists, and magicians such as James Randi, as well as exparapsychologists such as Susan Blackmore, are skeptical about the possibility of scientific controls for such factors. Parapsychological researchers, on the other hand, maintain that fraud on the part of investigators can be minimized by peer review, and that this has been successful in invalidating the reports of some researchers. For example, the work of the British parapsychologist, S.G. Soal, after peer review, was exposed for manipulating data.

Fraud on the part of *subjects* could perhaps be minimized by the presence of expert mentalists (stage performers specializing in "mind-reading") and other magicians, who would be able to detect mind-reading tricks, manipulations mimicking PK, and other tools in a magician's repertoire by which a purported "psychic" might be able to fool even professional scientists. A few parapsychologists have collaborated with magicians, and in the U.K. the Universities of Edinburgh and Hertfordshire have incorporated magicians into their parapsychological curriculum.

The question about causality. If and when the issue of the existence of certain psychic powers has been answered affirmatively, the question about the *cause* of such powers would still remain. American researchers, focusing intently in recent decades on the question of the existence of Psi, have, because of this concentration, postponed efforts to determine the *source* of such powers. If we could determine the cause, we presumably might be better able to train people to have these powers and/or provide the proper environment for those who do have psychic powers, and enlist the services of psychics for the benefit of mankind—for example, by helping police detectives to solve crimes or find missing persons.

The paradox of "normality." Abilities such as clairvoyance and telepathy are characterized as *para*normal precisely because they are considered to be non-natural, outside the bounds of human nature and its normal functioning. They seem to go against some of the "Basic Limiting Principles" listed by C.D. Broad, to which all natural events must conform: 1) A future event can't affect something in the present; 2) thoughts cannot be transmitted directly from one person's mind to another, without mediation of the senses; 3) it is impossible to move or affect external objects directly simply through a mental act; and 4) remote external objects can't be perceived without direct sensory contact. On the other hand, *if* the existence of such abilities were verified to the satisfaction of professional observers, and traced to some source, especially some physical source, the categorization of them as "paranormal" would no longer be relevant. Some natural cause would have been discovered, and perhaps even harnessed so that many "normal" persons could develop psychic powers.

Special problems with precognition. Some debate exists as to whether precognition implies the actual perception of future events, or the perception of the *possibility* of these future events. Some precognitive psychics maintain that they foresee only future possibilities, and that these possibilities can be altered through present actions—for example, a future accident or danger might be avoided by taking preventative measures in the present. But if precognition were defined as the *present* perception of *actual* future events, a revision of our concept of perception (which, by definition, is concerned with present objects or events) would be required, and likewise a revision of the concept of temporality, insofar as the future is by definition separate in a temporal series from the present, and not a possible object of conscious present perception.

The mind-body problematic. The difference between monistic and dualistic interpretations of the human psyche was discussed in Chapter 6. A monistic-*materialist* parapsychologist, who disbelieves in the existence of a mind separate and distinct from the brain, would necessarily have to look for a physical cause or causes of Psi if the existence of Psi was ascertained. Possible physical causes for telepathy might include low-frequency microwaves transmitted to subjects with a sensitivity to such waves; physical explanations such as geomagnetic and sunspot activity, alterations of barometric pressure, etc., have also been hypothesized as causes of various ESP phenomena. A monistic-*idealist* parapsychologist, who does not accept the reality of the material world, would look elsewhere—perhaps toward a network of minds that could be accessed by at least some persons, or toward some common "collective" mind in which all individuals participate. A dualist parapsychologist, however, would have more flexibility in possible approaches: He or she could explore the possibility of a physical cause such as microwaves, received by the body and interpreted by the mind; or, if William James' analogy (in the epigraph to this chapter) of trees commingling their roots became the new model or paradigm, the dualist might hypothesize the participation of the individual mind in a collective mind, transmissions from which could be more accessible to some individuals than to others. According to this dualist-collective model, telepathy might be explained by the fact that one individual's thoughts were picked up either directly or through some material medium by the collective mind and transmitted either directly or through material causes to an individual "receiver."

Any verification of "paranormal" abilities would require redefinition of "normality." This might entail major revisions of our standard notions of the mind and the various sense powers—a "paradigm shift" in the science of psychology. If the parameters of the "normal" were expanded, scientists who have very specific ideas about what is natural or normal might be expected to resist such revisions, even if confronted with persuasive evidence.

Awareness of such implications from the redefinition of the "standard psychological constants" may partially explain the ongoing diffidence and hesitation by many in the scientific community about supporting serious investigation of Psi. On the other hand, scientific paradigms do change—Newtonian physics giving way to relativity theory, cosmic "ether" as a medium giving way to electromagnetic theory, and so on. It is not inconceivable that psychological "givens" as to what can be perceived, or what sort of effects humans can have on material objects, will be revised to include something of what is at present designated "paranormal."

12

Survival After Death

SOCRATES: When the dead arrive at the place to which the genius [guardian spirit] of each severally guides them, first of all, they submit themselves to judgment, as they have lived well and piously or not. . . . Those who have been pre-eminent for holiness of life are released from this earthly prison, and go to their pure home which is above, and dwell on the true earth; and of these, such as have duly purified themselves with philosophy live henceforth altogether without the body, in mansions fairer still, which are not easily to be described.

—PLATO, *Phaedo*

Mind . . . seems to be a widely different kind of soul [from animal souls], differing as what is eternal from what is perishable; it alone is capable of existence in isolation from all other psychic powers. . . . When mind is set free from its present conditions it appears as just what it is and nothing more: this alone is immortal and eternal (we do not, however, remember its former activity because, while mind in this sense is impassible, mind as passive [including memory] is destructible), and without it nothing thinks.

—ARISTOTLE, *De anima* II:2, III:5

We feel and know that we are eternal.

—SPINOZA, *Ethics.*

In the Last Will and Testament of James Kidd, dated 2nd January, 1946, in Phoenix, Arizona, approximately a half-million dollars was willed to anyone who would do research to prove (preferably with a photograph) that the soul left the body at death. Kidd was declared missing and presumed dead in 1949. After Kidd's will was probated, 133 claimants fought in court for the research grant; the court trial is described in the book, *The Great Soul Trial*. The grant was finally awarded in 1971 to the American Society for Psychical Research, and the funds were used up by 1975. The American Society for Psychical Research unfortunately did not produce any scientific proof for the exit of the soul at death. If they had been successful, this chapter would be superfluous!

12.1 Initial Prejudices

In Chapter 2, we discussed the possibility that our prejudices may make it difficult or impossible to give an impartial answer to the question about the existence of specific human instincts. With regard to the present question, concerning survival after death, our prejudices may be even more intense, preventing us from coming to a cool and objective conclusion on the issue:

(1) Our natural fear of giving up our loved ones forever, being separated forever, and the idea of eternal separation being too painful for us to bear, may lead us to project our mere wish for a reunion into an expected reality.

(2) Our heightened sense of the value of personality—the idea that each person is of infinite worth and not expendable—can prevent us from accepting the idea that personality can just disintegrate, along with the body, at death.

(3) Subjectively, it is difficult or impossible for many of us to imagine our own annihilation; in the images we have of our future dissolution, our minds are still lurking in the background, observing the disintegration; or else the absence we are visualizing is the absence of our specific personality (so we are still there *negatively* in the images, as a missing factor).

Finally, (4) if we are unhappy with our lot in life or have a growing sense of the injustice in the world, it is natural to look for some counterbalance in the afterlife—a heaven in which individuals will finally be rewarded for their good deeds and injustices will finally be righted. We see good people snatched by death at an early age, bad people reaping all sorts of advantages that are undeserved; we hear about mass starvation, massacres and slaughters of vast numbers of people in various parts of the world; and we know from historians that in the twentieth century alone the combined total of deaths of innocent people caused by Hitler, Stalin, and Mao Zedong approximates one hundred million. It is natural to come to the conclusion that no justice exists in the world unless there is an afterlife, with rewards and punishments.

And so, for any or all of these reasons, many of us have belief in, and a hope for, the possibility of survival after death. But are there any reliable grounds for this belief and hope?

12.2 The Experimental Evidence: NDEs?

In discussing issues such as the mind-body problem, freedom, and love, in previous chapters, our starting point frequently was certain experiences that we have in common. But for obvious reasons there are obstacles to starting with our *personal* experience of death. In fact, it may be a misnomer to call death an "experience" at all, since experience presupposes life and consciousness. But since the question of our survival of death is an important question, in lieu of an experience in the strict sense, we will consider an experience about which much has been researched and written in the last few decades—the "near-death experience" (NDE). This experience has the advantage of being a *bona fide* experience recounted by a living person; but also has the disadvantage of not being a *bona fide* experience of death, since the person relating it has come back from a near encounter with death.

According to a 1991 Gallup poll, five percent of Americans—almost sixteen million people in the U.S.—claim to have had NDEs. Of the actual reports of NDEs, as judged from hospital records by a team of physicians, approximately one-third of these reports represent cases in which the near-death experiencers (NDEers) were actually clinically dead and had to be resuscitated. Obviously, the large number of NDEs in our time is related to the fact that artificial resuscitation instruments have been invented and are widely available; but accounts of cases in which persons died and came back to life with stories of unusual experiences also exist from ancient and medieval times.

The basic pattern of the experience (a summary of aspects often found in "deeper" NDEs) was first described by Raymond Moody, M.D., in his book *Life after Life*: After "dying," persons begin to hear various noises, for example, buzzing or ringing sounds, which are usually described as irritating or discomforting. Then they feel themselves moving through a long enclosure such as a tunnel, a cylinder, or a "valley." They notice that they can see their own traumatized physical body from a distance, and notice also that they still have a kind of ethereal "body" with the general outlines of head and extremities, but without specific physical features such as hair, fingernails, or wrinkles. Then they are met by friends or relatives who have died, and ultimately by a kindly "being of light" who conveys a few probing thoughts inviting them to reflect on their life. Then a long series of quite vivid "flashbacks" begins, starting with significant childhood experiences and leading up to more recent events; and with the help of the "being of light" they make evaluations of, and draw conclusions from, these flashbacks. Finally, some sort of "limit" or boundary line is reached (for example, a fence, a shore, a line, a bank of fog) that apparently divides this life from something else (perhaps another life?). By this time, the NDEers are usually filled with a sense of peace and contentment and are reluctant to return to their former life; but for some reason they either decide or are persuaded to return, or suddenly find themselves back in their former body.

Examining this pattern, we notice the following things: (1) It differs from many ancient and medieval stories of return from death, insofar as the experiences are typically quite positive, with very few "hellish" experiences, while ancient and medieval experiences were often frightening, with possibilities of eternal damnation. This has led some Christian commentators to regard them as unreliable, or even diabolical productions, making people think they don't have to worry about punishment in the afterlife. (But Maurice Rawlings, an evangelical Christian physician, in *Beyond Death's Door* and *To Hell and Back*, has discovered hellish experiences frequently, and the research of the International Association for Near-Death Studies (IANDS) at Yale University Medical Center have collected a considerable number of negative experiences.) Further investigations by other researchers have concluded that (2) not all NDEers enter into the deeper stages; (3) only a few actually sense that they have an ethereal body; (4) persons from different cultures, such as Hindus and Buddhists, tend to see environments more reflective of their cultures, and the "being of light" may be construed as Buddha, Shiva, or angels; and (5) after the experience, the NDEer quite often feels transformed, committed to growth in love, and no longer afraid of death. Skeptics tend to explain such experiences as hallucinatory, or caused by oxygen deprivation, lack of coordination of elements in the brain, the sudden increase of endorphins as a response to the pain of nearly dying, or special neurological responses that take place as the body begins to shut down its operations. However, some researchers maintain that these explanations are not sufficient to explain all phases of an intense NDE.

Since Moody's examination of NDE phenomena in the 1970s, scientific studies of NDE experiences have been conducted by psychologist Kenneth Ring, physician Michael Sabom, and others; and the *Journal of Near-Death Studies* (formerly called *Anabiosis*) has been published by the International Association for Near-Death Studies to document and analyze cases. The validity and meaning of alleged NDEs is subject to continuing debate; no "smoking gun" proofs that an individual actually separated from the body and returned to life have been produced.

What conclusion can *we* draw from the NDE?

(1) It doesn't provide evidence for survival after death, because those who experience it don't really finally die;

(2) even if they did verifiably die, and came back to us relating their experiences of "the other side," we could be skeptical of the validity of their experience, especially since we have had no such experience, or we may be doubtful of the veracity of their descriptions;

On the other hand, (3) the NDE does raise for us the interesting possibility that death, far from being painful, is one of the most delightful experiences possible;

(4) since no notoriously evil persons have had the positive NDEs, it may provide an incentive to others to avoid evil, just in case these experiences are an indication of what happens only to good people when they die!

and (5) it offers some interesting support to the dualistic interpretation of the mind-body relationship, especially in view of the comprehensive experiences that have taken place in an individual pronounced clinically dead.

12.3 Philosophical Analysis

Possibility versus actuality. By definition, philosophical discussions of survival after death have to do with possibility rather than actuality. An "afterlife" for an individual is construed as a future state, and arguments are made for or against the possibility of a state, concerning which no one can have present experience. But it is possible that the problem is not posed correctly. For if "eternal life" is something that begins in this present life, and can be experienced here and now, or seen "through a glass darkly" (*I Corinthians* 13:12), the question might be differently formulated. A religious person, for example, may claim that his or her faith offers direct and indubitable evidence of eternal life as a state of consciousness which transcends time—an actual experience to which those without faith may not have access. But on the level of purely rational analysis we must limit discussion to the issue of the *possibility* of future survival.

Logical possibility. In Chapter 7, logical possibility, which characterizes anything that is not self-contradictory, was discussed as one source for our concept of free choice. Logical possibility includes many things that fit into the category of things that are "possible, but not probable." For example, "it might rain tomorrow" although today is a clear day in the desert; or "I might receive an inheritance from a distant relative in another country" although I don't know of any such relative. Plato's theory about the pre-existence of the soul in heaven before it was implanted in a body, and released at death, and other theories of reincarnation, support survival after death as a logical possibility; they are arguing, in effect, that souls may be completely independent of the body, and can be put into or taken out of bodies, so that death is not really a disintegration of personality.

Some extremely imaginative contemporary physicists and cosmologists theorize that there are multiple dimensions besides the dimensions of space and time, and that the self is a complex of information like a massive computer program that can be translated into other levels, just as a symphony can be transposed into a musical score on paper, or into someone's memory, or into a computer program. The computer containing the program for a musical score may disintegrate, but the program can be run in another computer. Immortality thus would consist in reconstituting the essential "program" (the DNA?) which constitutes your self and your personality in some other sphere or level or dimension. Science-fiction writers, not to be outdone, have developed imaginative "Star Trek" scenarios based on the logical possibility of dematerializing personalities in a teleportation apparatus and reconstituting them in other spaces or dimensions.

Ontological possibility, however, goes beyond mere logical possibility. It is concerned with a real "potency" or "potential" or "power." For example, a gifted musician has not just the bare logical possibility, but the *potential*, of producing an electrifying performance; humans have the power of conceptualizing abstract universals, including ideas like "infinity"; mathematical geniuses have the ability or power of squaring multiple-digit numbers in their head in a few seconds; antibiotics have the potential of combating infectious diseases. All of these examples go well beyond the "possible, but not probable" category. Aristotle's theory of the soul similarly emphasizes ontological possibility: according to Aristotle, some operations of the mind exist which are not dependent on the body's sensation and imagination, and this intellectual part of the soul does not die with the body. Aristotle unfortunately was vague about what kind of survival this intellectual part would have; later medieval commentators came to opposite conclusions about this—St. Thomas Aquinas argued that the surviving intellect would be individualized, while the Arabian commentator on Aristotle, Averroes, hypothesized that it would be a communal intellect shared by the humans who happen to be living, and remaining after the deaths of individuals who participate in it.

Aside from the question of whether Aquinas's or Averroes's interpretation of Aristotle is correct, the basis of Aristotle's theory, and possibly the strongest conceptual argument for survival, is the existence of some mental operations that seem to take place independently of the body. Whether we agree or not with Aristotle may depend on whether we find in our own experience evidence of conscious activities which do not depend on an input of sensory data or constructs of the imagination. We may ask where an abstract idea like "human nature" comes from, since no one has ever seen or experienced a particular human nature; or how we can form the idea of infinity when there are no *actual* infinities in the world; or, if some person experiences sudden and unexplainable inspirations, or ESP, or out-of-body experiences (OBEs), we might ask where these come from.

However, an unavoidable difficulty is connected with the Aristotelian approach. In the Aristotelian formulation, the soul is the "form" of the body. Our usual notions of an afterlife presuppose a separation of a soul from the body. But since a form can presumably not exist separated from some "content," Christian scholastics and Aristotelian philosophers have had difficulty explaining how the soul as pure form could survive bodily death, and how, if it did survive, it could be conscious at all, without at least some input or content from the senses.

In order to avoid problems of a form existing in the afterlife with no content, or an unconscious separated soul-form, some early Christian Fathers and philosophers, such as Origen and

Plotinus, favored an "astral body" hypothesis, according to which everyone has a semi-spiritual or ethereal body that exists together with their physical body but is released at death; so that "death" would be just the disappearance of the outer shell, while the individual person *and* his/her ethereal body survives. Variations of this theory are found in Eastern religions, including Hinduism and Buddhism. The *Tibetan Book of the Dead* offers a detailed analysis of what happens to the astral body after bodily death.

12.4 Conclusions Regarding Immortality

As indicated above, in spite of James Kidd's generous bequest for research, no convincing *empirical* proof of survival is available. NDEs offer some intriguing clues that survival takes place, especially if no satisfactory physiological or psychological explanation is forthcoming. But they do not at present constitute a proof of survival. The best chance for authentication of NDEs might be if congenitally blind individuals actually reported visual experiences, as some cases report, or if congenitally deaf individuals accurately reported sounds. Some researchers, in order to acquire empirical evidence from NDEs, have placed randomly changing displays on ledges in operating rooms, in case a patient floating upward might be able to read these displays and thus offer credible proof that he or she had been really hovering above their body before resuscitation. This experiment has not produced any significant results. However, even if a resuscitated patient could afterwards recount what was on the display at the time of their clinical death, a skeptic might attribute this to ESP, if not to fraud on the part of those who reported the incident. And to the skeptical mind, not even the ghostly apparition of a definitely dead person would be conclusive proof of survival.

A *metaphysical* approach, utilizing purely rational and conceptual analysis may focus on the fact that certain mental or spiritual operations do not appear to be dependent on the senses or bodily organs. This realization may facilitate the transition (for a metaphysician) from "logical possibility" of survival to a conviction of a real potency or capability. This conviction is unavoidably dependent on *subjective* experience and interpretation. But "subjective" does not necessarily mean "illusory." Just as the researchers in the Manhattan project in 1942 were able to accurately predict a future atomic bomb from their experiments with self-sustaining chain reactions, so also individuals on the basis of personal intellectual or spiritual experiences independent of bodily conditions, may consistently project a future continuation of at least that area of personality undergoing these experiences.

12.5 Immortality versus Resurrection

Immortality is a philosophical concept. Pre-Christian philosophers such as Plato and Aristotle, who had no notion of bodily resurrection, accepted the idea of immortality, as a logical possibility or as a real ontological power or capability existing in individuals. Resurrection, on the other hand, is a *religious* belief, emphasized especially in Christianity with its unique beliefs in the incarnation of God as a human being, the death and resurrection of Jesus, and the promise that the dead "shall arise from the tomb" (*John* 5:28), and St. Paul's more detailed description:

> All of us are to be changed—in an instant, in the twinkling of an eye, at the sound of the last trumpet. The trumpet will sound and the dead will be raised incorruptible, and we shall be changed. This corruptible body must be clothed with incorruptibility, this mortal body with immortality. (*1 Corinthians* 15:51–53)

The Christian emphasis on bodily resurrection is exemplified in canonization processes in the Roman Catholic tradition, in which one frequent stage in the investigation of a candidate for sainthood is the exhumation of his or her remains to see if they have resisted corruption. Incorrupt remains, as described in Joan Cruz's *The Incorruptibles*, are taken by some to be a miraculous presage of a future resurrection for all.

12.6 Special Problems with Resurrection

The *resurrection of Jesus*, as reported in the Gospels, appears to involve some contradictions. On the one hand, in the appearance

of Jesus in his resurrected body to the Apostles, he comes instan-
taneously into a room which was locked because of the Apostles'
fear of arrest (*John* 20:19, 26); and on another occasion, while
walking and talking with some disciples and being "changed in
appearance" (*Mark* 16:12), he suddenly disappears (*Luke* 24:31).
Such accounts seem to imply that Jesus's body was no longer subject to material laws. On the other hand, he also has his feet
grasped by the two Marys after rising (*Matthew* 28:9), eats some
food after his resurrection, apparently to prove that his body was
real (*Luke* 24:41–43), invites all the apostles to touch him, to
prove that he is not a ghost (*Luke* 24:39), and even invites the
Apostle Thomas to put his finger in the place in his hands where
the nails were and his hand in the place in his side where a lance
made a gash (*John* 20:27). If no contradiction is involved, one can
only conclude that Jesus's body would have to be unlike any other
body in our experience. Perhaps the closest analogy would be science-fiction stories in which space warriors use futuristic technology to de-materialize and be re-materialized in other galaxies; the
difference here is that no machine is involved. St. Paul in *I
Corinthians* 15:49, trying to explain the nature of the resurrected
body, describes it as a "spiritual body," which on a purely rational
level would be an oxymoron.

The *resurrection of individuals*, believers or unbelievers, good
or bad, presents an even greater philosophical challenge than the
resurrection of Jesus, if we take into account the fact that it would
involve the reconstitution of bodies that have disintegrated,
become fertilizer for plants, been eaten by animals or other
humans, been cremated, and had ashes tossed over the ocean.
Scientists tell us that atoms and molecules are constantly being
replaced in our bodies; so we can speculate about resurrection as a
massive replacement, perhaps utilizing a template, mold, or
records of DNA to construct a "spiritual body." On the other
hand, no reconstitution may be necessary if the "astral body"
hypothesis, discussed above, is correct, and if the astral body could
be empowered to materialize at will.

Although resurrection is universally believed by Christians, not
all Christians believe in immortality! Various Christian "heretics"

have maintained that the idea of immortality is a pagan notion, propounded by Plato in his *Phaedo,* while true immortality or resurrection is a supernatural gift bestowed by God on those who are faithful. According to some variations, nonbelievers or sinners will be completely annihilated at death. In the aftermath of the Protestant Reformation, the idea of some reformers that humans are not naturally immortal was condemned by the Catholic Church at the Lateran Council of 1513:

> Whereas some have dared to assert concerning the nature of the reasonable soul that it is mortal, we, with the approbation of the sacred council do condemn and reprobate all those who assert that the intellectual soul is mortal, seeing, according to the canon of Pope Clement V, that the soul is . . . immortal . . . and we decree that all who adhere to like erroneous assertions shall be shunned and punished as heretics.

12.7 A Final Possibility

Without taking sides in this resurrection-immortality controversy, we might take the present opportunity to point out that the term, "possibility," has another signification that has not yet been considered in this chapter—a *psychological* meaning, somewhat similar to faith, but broader than the religious connotations of "faith."

Belief, in many cases, is related to reality in the sense that it is a prerequisite to a reality, or makes that reality possible or achievable. In situations where humans have objectives or goals, belief is often necessary to actualize the possibilities. For example, we can surmise that the athlete who doesn't believe he or she can break an Olympic record will not be able to do so, and will not even try to do so; while an athlete who believes he or she can do it at least opens up that possibility and may even achieve the goal; similarly, a student who has no belief in his or her ability to pass a calculus course, will definitely be unable to do so; while the believing student may have that possibility. If we follow a parallel line of thought, the materialist who doesn't believe in free will as a possibility (see Chapter 7) will, just because of this skepticism, be subjected to necessities of heredity and environment, and never exercise free will! Likewise, perhaps the unbeliever who holds that

death is the end of each individual will come to a complete dissolution just because of that belief. In any case, the believing individual may have a tactical advantage, as Rabbi Y.M. Tukachinsky
once pointed out in a parable:

> Twin brothers, fetuses in their mother's womb, enjoyed a carefree life.
> Their world was dark and warm and protected. These twins were alike
> in all aspects but one. One brother was a 'believer': he believed in an
> afterlife, in a future reality much different from their current, minia-
> ture universe.
>
> The second brother, however, was a skeptic. All he knew was the
> familiar world of the womb. Anything besides what he could feel and
> sense was only an illusion. The skeptic tried to talk some sense into his
> brother. He warned him to be realistic, but to no avail. His naive
> brother insisted on believing in an extraordinary world that exists after
> life in the womb, a world so immense and fantastic that it transcends
> their wildest imaginings.
>
> The months passed, and the fatal moment arrived. Labor began.
> The fetuses became aware of tremendous contractions and shifting in
> their little world. The freethinker recognized that 'this is it'. His short
> but pleasant life was about to end. He felt the forces pressuring him
> to go down, but fought against them. He knew that outside the
> womb, a cruel death awaited, with no protective sack and no umbili-
> cal cord. Suddenly, he realized that his naive brother was giving in to
> the forces around them. He was sinking lower!
>
> "Don't give up!" he cried, but his brother took no heed. "Where
> are you, my dear brother?" He shuddered as he heard his brother's
> screams from outside the womb. His poor brother had met his cruel
> fate. How naive he had been, with his foolish belief in a bigger, bet-
> ter world!
>
> Then the skeptic felt the uterine muscles pushing him out,
> against his will, into the abyss. He screamed out . . .
>
> "Mazal Tov!" called out the doctor. "Two healthy baby boys!"
> (Cited at http://www.geocities.com/m_yericho/ravkook/EMOR58
> .htm)

With this question we reach the furthest horizons of our understanding of human nature. Peering into these horizons, we can
contemplate possibilities of surviving in an astral body, or being

transported to another dimension, or entering into a state of repose waiting for a supernatural restoration in the form of a "spiritual body." Our psychological belief may also be a factor in opening up these possibilities. But rational investigation has not proceeded any further than this. Religious faith, however, may carry some persons further to a type of certainty that cannot be attained at present by philosophical speculation about logical or ontological possibilities.

Solutions Fitting Problems

The characteristics of solutions correspond to the characteristics of the subject-matter being considered. A detective trying to track down someone who has committed a crime may be satisfied with identifying fingerprints or DNA matches; a mathematician interested in finding out how many prime numbers are in a finite series may be satisfied when he gets a reliable computer response to his query; a paleontologist interested in locating missing links from the Cambrian era may feel satisfied in carbon-dating some fossils from that era. But the subjects we have been considering are much more complex than the problems of mathematics or the physical sciences, since they bring in multiple subjective aspects necessarily omitted in order to arrive at objective results in these other disciplines. We should not be surprised if the results that emerge are complex and paradoxical.

For example, a "straightforward" solution to the question, "what is the difference between human beings and the other animals" would be in the form, "the essential difference-in-kind is X," where "X" might be rationality, or the ability to make tools. But as we have seen, all of these common answers are subject to challenges. The most impregnable conclusion—self-consciousness as the chief human difference—is paradoxical, insofar as, while it may be the most obvious to us as a clear-cut difference-in-kind, it is the least objectively observable and provable difference.

Numerous other paradoxes have been encountered in the other issues we have considered, including the following:

- The exclusively human instinct may be to rationalize or deny all human instincts

- The best way to understand and maximize hereditary endowments may be to allow maximum environmental mobility.

- The emphasis on the difference of male from female may be the major differentiating characteristic of males.

- The final unification of the human race may require its ultimate diversification.

- Human beings are both a unity *and* a duality between mind and body, body and soul.

- Political freedom involves the free creation of institutions that limit freedom.

- Child development is an impetus by necessity toward freedom.

- Maturity, far from being a stable state of equilibrium finally reached at a certain point in human development, is the constant oscillation between extremes.

- The best response to the ancient question, "Is love between opposites or between similars?" is that it is a unity absolutely requiring diversity.

- The scientifically acceptable verification of paranormal phenomena would put them into the category of the "normal."

- Belief in immortality may be the prerequisite to attaining it, while disbelief may be a self-fulfilling prophecy.

Sometimes the complaint is made that philosophers have been considering issues such as the ones in this book for thousands of years, and, unlike the scientists, have not come to a consensus on one single issue. One reason for this may be that philosophers, like the scientists, characteristically try to avoid paradoxes. But contemplating this state of affairs, we arrive at one final paradox: A complex (paradoxical) solution may be the simplest solution to a complex problem (like the characteristics of human nature); while an overhasty or oversimplified "solution" may result in obfuscation or confusion. At least one of the effects of our investigation should be a greater appreciation of the complexity and multiple facets of human nature.

Selected Bibliography

Chapter 1: The "Difference" Question

Adler, Mortimer. *The Difference of Man and the Difference It Makes.* Cleveland: Meridian, 1967.

Candland, Douglas. *Feral Children and Clever Animals.* New York: Oxford University Press, 1993.

Premack, David. *Gavagai! Or the Future History of the Animal Language Controversy.* Cambridge, Massachusetts: MIT Press, 1986.

Rumbaugh, Duane, and Timothy Gill. Language and the Acquisition of Language-Type Skills by a Chimpanzee. *Annals of the New York Academy of Science* 270 (April 28th, 1976).

Savage-Rumbaugh, Sue, et al. *Apes, Language, and the Human Mind.* New York: Oxford University Press, 1998.

———. *Language Comprehension in Ape and Child.* Chicago: University of Chicago Press, 1993.

Sebeok, Thomas, and Umiker-Sebeok, Jean. *Speaking of Apes: A Critical Anthology of Two-Way Communication with Man.* New York: Plenum, 1980.

Temerlin, Marice. *Lucy: Growing Up Human.* Palo Alto: Science and Behavior, 1972.

Terrance, Herbert S. What I Learned from Nim Chimsky. In Stuart Hirschberg and Terry Hirschberg, eds., *Reflections on Language* (New York: Oxford University Press, 1999).

Wallman, Joel. *Aping Language.* New York: Cambridge University Press, 1992.

Chapter 2: Are There Any Distinctively Human Instincts?

Fletcher, Ronald. *Instinct in Man*. New York: International Universities Press, 1968.

Jung, Carl G. *Modern Man in Search of a Soul*. New York: Vintage, 1965.

Lorenz, Konrad. *King Solomon's Ring: New Light on Animal Ways*. Translated by Marjorie Kerr Wilson. New York: Crowell, 1952.

Lyons, John. *Noam Chomsky*. New York: Penguin, 1978.

McGilvray, James. *The Cambridge Companion to Chomsky*. New York: Cambridge University Press, 2005.

Piattelli-Palmarini, Massimo, ed. *Language and Learning: The Debate between Jean Piaget and Noam Chomsky*. Cambridge, Massachusetts: Harvard University Press, 1980.

Pinker, Steven. *The Language Instinct*. New York: HarperPerennial, 1995.

Singer, June. *Boundaries of the Soul: The Practice of Jung's Psychology*. Revised and updated. New York: Anchor, 1994.

Smith, N.V. *Chomsky: Ideas and Ideals*. New York: Cambridge University Press, 1999.

Stein, Murray. *Jung's Map of the Soul: An Introduction*. Chicago: Open Court, 1998.

Chapter 3: Can Personality Traits and Intelligence Be Inherited?

Alford, John, et al. Are Political Orientations Genetically Transmitted? *American Political Science Review* (May 2005).

American Psychological Association. Intelligence Task Force Report, 1996, http://www.indiana.edu/~intell/apa96.shtml.

Bartholomew, David. *Measuring Intelligence: Facts and Fallacies*. New York: Cambridge University Press, 2004.

Bishop, Jerry, and Michael Waldholz. *Genome: The Story of the Most Astonishing Scientific Adventure of Our Time—The Attempt to Map All the Genes in the Human Body*. New York: Simon and Schuster, 1990.

Dagg, Anne Innis. *"Love of Shopping" Is Not a Gene: Problems with Darwinian Psychology*. New York: Black Rose, 2005.

Dawkins, Richard. *The Selfish Gene*. Second edition. New York: Oxford University Press, 1989.

Dobzhansky, Theodosius. *Mankind Evolving: The Evolution of the Human Species.* New Haven: Yale University Press, 1962.

Flynn, James R. *What Is Intelligence? Beyond the Flynn Effect.* New York: Cambridge University Press, 2007.

Gander, Eric. *On Our Minds: How Evolutionary Psychology Is Reshaping the Nature-Nurture Debate.* Baltimore: Johns Hopkins University Press, 2003.

Gould, Stephen Jay. *The Mismeasure of Man.* New York: Norton, 1996.

Herrnstein, Richard, and Charles Murray. *The Bell Curve: Intelligence and Class Structure in American Life.* New York: Simon and Schuster, 1996.

Jacoby, Russell, and Naomi Galuberman, eds. *The Bell Curve Debate : History, Documents, Opinions.* New York: Times Books, 1995.

Jensen, Arthur. *The g Factor: The Science of Mental Ability.* Westport: Praeger, 1998.

Konner, Melvin. *The Tangled Wing: Biological Constraints on the Human Spirit.* New York: Harper and Row, 1983.

Ornstein, Robert. *The Roots of the Self: Unraveling the Mystery of Who We Are.* San Francisco: Harper, 1993.

Thompson, Paul. *Issues in Evolutionary Ethics.* Albany: State University of New York Press, 1995.

Toman, Walter. *Family Constellation.* New York: Springer, 1976.

White, Elliot, ed. *Intelligence, Political Inequality, and Public Policy.* Westport: Praeger, 1997.

Wicherts, Jelte, et al. Are Intelligence Tests Measurement Invariant over Time? Investigating the Nature of the Flynn Effect. *Intelligence* 32:5 (2004).

Wilson, Edward O. *On Human Nature.* Cambridge, Massachusetts: Harvard University Press, 1978.

Chapter 4: Are There Any Signigicant Sex-Related Personality Chatacteristics?

Archer, John, and Barbara Lloyd. *Sex and Gender.* New York: Cambridge University Press, 1985.

Baron-Cohen, Simon. *The Essential Difference: The Truth about the Male and Female Brain.* New York: Basic Books, 2003.

Blum, Deborah. *Sex on the Brain: The Biological Differences Between Men and Women.* New York: Penguin, 1997.

Buckingham-Hatfield, Susan. *Gender and Environment.* New York: Routledge, 2000.

Caplan, Paula, et al. *Gender Differences in Human Cognition*. New York: Oxford University Press, 1997.

Christen, Yves. *Sex Differences: Modern Biology and the Unisex Fallacy*. Translated by Nicholas Davidson. New Brunswick: Transaction, 1991.

Fischer, Agneta. *Gender and Emotion: Social Psychological Perspectives*. New York: Cambridge University Press, 2000.

Gilmore, David. *Manhood in the Making: Cultural Concepts of Masculinity*. New Haven: Yale University Press, 1990.

Keller, Evelyn Fox. *Reflections on Gender and Science*. New Haven: Yale University Press, 1985.

Lloyd, Genevieve. *The Man of Reason: "Male" and "Female" in Western Philosophy*. Minneapolis: University of Minnesota Press, 1984.

Harding, Sandra, and Merrill B. Hintikka, eds. *Discovering Reality: Feminist Perspectives on Epistemology, Metaphysics, Methodology, and Philosophy of Science*. Boston: Kluwer, 2003.

Storkey, Elaine. *Origins of Difference: The Gender Debate Revisited*. Grand Rapids: Baker Academic, 2001.

Tannen, Deborah. *You Just Don't Understand: Woman and Men in Conversation*. New York: Ballantine, 1991.

Tavris, Carol. *The Mismeasure of Woman*. New York: Touchstone, 1992.

Tavris, Carol, and Carol Offir. *The Longest War: Sex Differences in Perspective*. New York: Harcourt, Brace, 1977.

Walsh, Mary Roth, ed. *Women, Men, and Gender: Ongoing Debates*. New Haven: Yale University Press, 1997.

Williamson, Marianne. *A Woman's Worth*. New York: Random House, 1993.

Chapter 5: Human Evolution

Fabel, Arthur, and Donald St. John, eds. *Teilhard in the Twenty-First Century: The Emerging Spirit of Earth*. Maryknoll: Orbis, 2003.

Jaynes, Julian. *The Origins of Consciousness in the Breakdown of the Bicameral Mind*. Boston: Houghton Mifflin, 1976.

Lévy, Pierre. *Collective Intelligence: Mankind's Emerging World in Cyberspace*. Translated by Robert Bononno. New York: Plenum, 1997.

McDermott, Ed. *The Essential Aurobindo*. Great Barrington: Lindisfarne, 2001.

McLuhan, Marshall. *Understanding Media: The Extensions of Man*. Critical edition, edited by Terrence Gordon. Corte Madera: Ginko, 2005.

Meynard, Thierry, S.J., ed. *Teilhard and the Future of Humanity*. New York: Fordham University Press, 2006.

O'Connell, Robert. *Teilhard's Vision of the Past: The Making of a Method*. New York: Fordham University Press, 1982.

Ornstein, Robert. *The Evolution of Consciousness: of Darwin, Freud, and Cranial Fire—The Origins of the Way We Think*. New York: Prentice Hall, 1991.

Taylor, Gordon Rattray. *The Great Evolution Mystery*. New York: Harper and Row, 1983.

Teilhard de Chardin, Pierre. *The Future of Man*. New York: Harper and Row, 1964.

———. *Human Energy*. New York: Harcourt, Brace, 1969.

———. *The Human Phenomenon*. Translated by Sarah Appleton-Weber. Portland: Sussex Academic Press, 1999.

———. *Towards the Future*. Translated by René Hague. New York: Harcourt, Brace, 1975.

Thomas, Lewis. *The Lives of a Cell: Notes of a Biology Watcher*. New York: Viking, 1974.

Chapter 6: Is Human Nature a Unity or a Duality?

Eccles, John. *Evolution of the Brain: Creation of the Self*. New York: Routledge, 1989.

Hook, Sidney. *Dimensions of Mind: A Symposium*. New York: New York University Press, 1960.

Johnson, Mark. *The Body in the Mind: The Bodily Basis of Meaning, Imagination, and Reason*. Chicago: University of Chicago Press, 1987.

Kirk, Robert. *Mind and Body*. Montreal: McGill-Queen's University Press, 2003.

Paterson, R.W.K. *Philosophy and the Belief in Life after Death*. New York: St. Martin's, 1995.

Popper, Karl R., and John Eccles. *The Self and its Brain*. New York: Springer, 1977.

Restak, Richard. *The Brain Has a Mind of Its Own: Insights from a Practicing Neurologist*. New York: Harmony, 1991.

Robert, Frank. *Passions within Reason: The Strategic Role of the Emotions*. New York: Norton, 1988.

Chapter 7: Human Freedom

Adler, Mortimer. *The Idea of Freedom.* Two volumes. Garden City: Doubleday, 1958–61.

Compton, Arthur. *The Freedom of Man.* New Haven: Yale University Press, 1935.

Dennett, Daniel. *Elbow Room: The Varieties of Free Will Worth Wanting.* Cambridge, Massachusetts: MIT Press, 1984.

Fischer, John Martin. *The Metaphysics of Free Will.* Oxford: Blackwell, 1994.

James, William. The Dilemma of Determinism. In Douglas Browning and William T. Myers, eds., *Philosophers of Process* (New York: Fordham University Press, 1998).

Rouner, Leroy, ed. *On Freedom.* Notre Dame: University of Notre Dame Press, 1989.

Chapter 8: Human Development

Boelen, Bernard. *Personal Maturity: The Existential Dimension.* New York: Seabury, 1978.

Caplan, Frank, ed. *The First Twelve Months of Life.* New York: Bantam, 1978.

Erikson, Erik. *Childhood and Society.* New York: Norton, 1985.

———. *Identity and the Life Cycle.* New York: Norton, 1980.

Ilg, Frances, and Louise Bates. *Child Behavior.* New York: Harper and Row, 1955.

Lerner, Richard. *Concepts and Theories of Human Development.* Mahwah: Erlbaum, 2002.

Piaget, Jean. *The Origins of Intelligence in Children.* New York: International Universities Press, 1966.

Russell, James, ed. *Philosophical Perspectives on Developmental Psychology.* New York: Blackwell, 1987.

Chapter 9: Maturity

Boelen, Bernard. *Personal Maturity: The Existential Dimension.* New York: Seabury, 1978.

Feibleman, James. *The Stages of Human Life.* The Hague: Nijhoff, 1975.

Gould, Roger. *Transformations.* New York: Simon and Schuster, 1978.

Hall, Douglas. *Career Development.* Brookfield: Dartmouth, 1994.

Levinson, Daniel. The Life Cycle. In H.I. Kaplan and B.J. Sadock, eds., *Comprehensive Textbook of Psychiatry*, fourth edition (Baltimore: Williams and Williams, 1985).

———. *The Seasons of a Man's Life.* New York: Ballantine, 1978.

———. *The Seasons of a Woman's Life.* New York: Knopf, 1996.

Lidz, Theodore. *The Person, His and Her Development Throughout the Life Cycle.* New York: Basic Books, 1976.

Ortega y Gasset, Jose. *Man and Crisis.* New York: Norton, 1958.

Sheehy, Gail. *New Passages.* New York: Random House, 1995.

———. *Pathfinders.* New York: Morrow, 1981.

Chapter 10: The Nature of Love

Brown, Robert. *Analyzing Love.* New York: Cambridge University Press, 1987.

Cowburn, John. *Love.* Milwaukee: Marquette University Press, 2003.

Freud, Sigmund. *Civilization and Its Discontents.* Translated by James Strachey. New York: Norton, 1962.

Lewis, C.S. *The Four Loves.* New York: Harcourt, Brace, 1988.

Norton, David, and Mary Kille. *Philosophies of Love.* Totowa: Rowman and Allanheld, 1983.

Schneider, Isidor. *The World of Love.* Volume 1. New York: Braziller, 1964.

Singer, Irving. *The Nature of Love.* Three volumes. Chicago: University of Chicago Press, 1984.

Soble, Alan. *The Structure of Love.* New Haven: Yale University Press, 1990.

Chapter 11: Philosophy and the Paranormal

Broughton, Richard. *Parapsychology: The Controversial Science.* New York: Ballantine, 1991.

Griffin, David Ray. *Parapsychology, Philosophy, and Spirituality: A Postmodern Exploration.* Albany: State University of New York Press, 1997.

Grim, Patrick, ed. *Philosophy of Science and the Occult.* Albany: State University of New York Press, 1982.

Krippner, Stanley, ed. *Advances in Parapsychological Research.* Jefferson: McFarland, 1997.

Rhine, J.B., and J.G. Pratt. *Parapsychology: Frontier Science of the Mind.* Springfield: Thomas, 1957.

Stokes, Douglas. *The Nature of Mind: Parapsychology and the Role of Consciousness in the Physical World.* Jefferson: McFarland, 1997.

Williams, Mary, ed. *Paranormal Phenomena: Opposing Viewpoints.* San Diego: Greenhaven, 2003.

Chapter 12: Survival After Death

Abanes, Richard. *Journey into the Light: Exploring Near-Death Experiences.* Grand Rapids: Baker, 1996.

Flew, Anthony. *Merely Mortal: Can You Survive Your Own Death?* Amherst: Prometheus, 2000.

Fox, Mark. *Religion, Spirituality, and the Near-Death Experience.* New York: Routledge, 2003.

Moody, Raymond. *Life after Life.* Atlanta: Mockingbird, 1975.

Paterson, R.W.K. *Philosophy and the Belief in a Life after Death.* New York: St. Martin's, 1995.

Rawlings, Maurice. *To Hell and Back.* Nashville: Nelson, 1996.

———. *Beyond Death's Door.* Nashville: Nelson, 1978.

Ring, Kenneth. *The Omega Project.* New York: Morrow, 1992.

Ring, Kenneth. *Life at Death: A Scientific Investigation of the Near-death Experience.* New York: Coward, McCann, and Geoghegan, 1980.

Sabom, Michael. *Light and Death: One Doctor's Fascinating Account of Near-Death Experiences.* Grand Rapids: Zondervan, 1998.

Toynbee, Arnold, Arthur Koestler, *et al*, eds. *Life after Death.* New York: McGraw-Hill, 1976.

Van Lommel, Pim, et al. Near-Death Experience in Survivors of Cardiac Arrest: A Prospective Study in the Netherlands. *Lancet* 2039–45, (2001).

Index